# A SERIOUS HOUSE

# A SERIOUS HOUSE

Why if Churches Fall Completely Out of Use,
We May Miss Them

MARTIN CAMROUX

*Foreword by David R. Peel*

WIPF & STOCK · Eugene, Oregon

A SERIOUS HOUSE
Why if Churches Fall Completely Out of Use, We May Miss Them

Copyright © 2024 Martin Camroux. All rights reserved. Except for brief quotations in critical publications or reviews, no part of this book may be reproduced in any manner without prior written permission from the publisher. Write: Permissions, Wipf and Stock Publishers, 199 W. 8th Ave., Suite 3, Eugene, OR 97401.

Wipf & Stock
An Imprint of Wipf and Stock Publishers
199 W. 8th Ave., Suite 3
Eugene, OR 97401

www.wipfandstock.com

PAPERBACK ISBN: 979-8-3852-0782-4
HARDCOVER ISBN: 979-8-3852-0783-1
EBOOK ISBN: 979-8-3852-0784-8

VERSION NUMBER 042524

# CONTENTS

*Foreword by David R. Peel* | vii
*Acknowledgements* | xi

1. Losing Sight of Church | 1
2. A Very Human Institution | 17
3. Sacred Space—A Symphony in Stone | 26
4. Jesus—No Story So Divine | 46
5. "What Life Have You If You Have Not Life Together?" | 69
6. The Church as Moral Community | 83
7. Lost in Wonder, Love, and Praise | 98
8. Gathered to Hear the Word | 122
9. Finding a Meaning for Life | 135
10. You Never Know What You've Got till It's Gone | 149

*Bibliography* | 165
*Index* | 173

# FOREWORD

Martin Camroux's social science background continues to aid his understanding of the context in which contemporary Christian ministry and service is now set. Early each year, Martin sends me a copy of his analysis and interpretation of the statistics taken from the annual United Reformed Church Year Book. It always makes depressing reading. Like other mainstream Western churches, the URC is hemorrhaging members year on year. Those lost to death are not being replaced, thereby reflecting an alarming absence of significant intergenerational continuity. The acids of secularization continue to eat away the ecclesial fabric which once adorned a confident Western Christendom. Church scandals have recently contributed to a once iconic institution's loss of standing in society: the custodians of the gospel treasure have time and again proved to be all too fallible vessels. Arguably, though, a primary failing of "confident Christendom" lay in the utopian and idealistic perception it had of itself: the seeds of decline often are sown in periods of success.

Martin is one of the church's more perceptive and persuasive critics. He is totally honest about its present plight, not least because when true to its *raison d'etre* it was a major contributor to his own nurture and development. Unlike some, his knowledge of the church's glaring imperfections has not caused him to give up on it. His vivid experience of its life-enhancing and kingdom-building potential drives him to point out in his latest book what would be lost if the churches finally succumbed to secularism. While wholeheartedly accepting that the church will have to reconfigure itself to meet the needs and opportunities thrown up by contemporary culture, in *A Serious House*, Martin lays out what he believes are the essential elements of a future faithful and relevant Christian community.

## FOREWORD

If a church is to carry a narrative which is intellectually credible, spiritually enhancing, and politically effective, any flirting with fundamentalism or settling for sectarianism must be eschewed. Those who maintain that getting rid of the church's real estate is the panacea for all ecclesial ills are invited by Martin to reflect upon the fact that many of today's "cultured despisers" (Schleiermacher) are seeking "spiritual spaces" which enable them to connect with the transcendent dimension of their seemingly one-dimensional world. The story of Jesus, which brought the Christian movement into being, remains the church's driving force. We know all too well, however, that very often church activities bear little explicit relation to it. The bedrock resources for the church's alternative narrative to that of consumerist, secular culture thereby often becomes silenced. In our passionate attempts to keep the show on the road at all costs we lose contact with the reasons why the church was originally brought into being. Martin insists that the creation of opportunities for people to experience the transcendent and encounter the Jesus we read about in the gospel tradition is central to the church's contemporary task. What the church points to and seeks to embody provides the means whereby how we understand ourselves becomes transformed, new life is encountered, and commitment to reshape society in kingdom-shaped ways is generated.

Martin stresses the centrality of worship in local congregations. It should be grounded in our response to God's gracious dealings with us, but very often it becomes distorted when in our hands it comes to resemble a performance put on to satisfy an audience. Martin has equally important things to say about preaching at a time when some in our media-dominated culture insist that the age does not suit the homiletic idiom. The quality of sermons, he insists, are the problem, not the preaching practice itself. Preachers are urged to work harder at their craft, thereby creating opportunities through their words for God to come alive in the minds and hearts of their hearers. Martin brings his extensive experience of small churches to the center of his missiological thinking. Faithfulness or relevance in the church does not depend upon the size of one's congregation: often small is indeed beautiful. What counts ultimately is a Christian community's wholehearted commitment to participate in worship, share its communal life, and exercise discipleship. Without such "essentials" churches are Christian in name only.

As we have come to expect, Martin's style draws readers into his argument through judicious use of quotations drawn from his extensive reading, not only in theology but also literature and poetry. *A Serious House* deserves a wide readership. It not only offers encouragement to disillusioned church members despairing about what has been happening to the church over many years, but it also challenges those who have given up on the church to reconsider their decision. The church's origin, shape, lifestyle, and destiny *ultimately* owe everything to God, re-presented to us in Jesus, and alive ever anew in the power of the Spirit. More widely, therefore, this book will be welcomed by those who share Martin's belief that the church is a community in which the question concerning the meaning, purpose, and destiny of life is raised, and an answer given in a Jesus-centered narrative; one that even leads to the reshaping in Christlike ways of the economic, social, and political realities of an unequal and unjust world.

# ACKNOWLEDGEMENTS

This is a very personal book, but it is hugely indebted to those who have stimulated my mind, challenged my ideas, and improved my grammar! Most of all my gratitude is to my wife, Margaret, who has read it all, encouraged me, and pointed out when even if I knew what I was trying to say no one else would. I am grateful to my children, Eleanor and Michael, who also put up with me and encouraged me. Eleanor has also read the whole text, improving, commenting, and demonstrating how much better her grammar is than mine.

I am hugely grateful to David Peel, the United Reformed Church's most distinguished living theologian, for reading and making detailed comments on all the chapters, with a theological depth which I lack and with the good humor and kindness which is typical of him. I am grateful also to Ian MacPherson, who I first met when he was the chaplain to congregational students at the University of Hull in the 1960s, and who also read and commented on all the chapters. I am grateful to David Cornick and to Clyde Binfield who read the completed manuscript and made helpful comments. David's suggestion that the personal elements of the book were the most interesting led to my rewriting the first two chapters.

Conversations of all kinds helped me shape my ideas and I am grateful among others to David Lawrence, who never failed to cogently challenge my ideas, to Tony Barnes, Geoffrey Gleed, Anne Lewitt, Iain MacDonald, and Roger Cooke. I am also indebted to Riverside Church, in the city of New York which, especially in the ministry of William Sloane Coffin, demonstrated what a church should be.

I am deeply grateful to the congregations in which I ministered, Freemantle United Reformed Church, Southampton; Trinity with Palm Grove URC/Methodist Church, Birkenhead; Immanuel United Reformed Church, Swindon; and Trinity United Reformed and Methodist Church in

## ACKNOWLEDGEMENTS

Sutton. I was fortunate that all of these had lively junior churches, choirs and organists who made worship special for me and a good selection of the saints of God. I am grateful to the ecumenical partners with whom I worked, who made ministry so much richer than if I had ministered simply in my own United Reformed Church. In the last ten years since retirement, I am grateful that I was able to preach nearly every Sunday, mostly in small country churches, or in larger urban churches now living out their ministries in more uncertain times. I am grateful to the Colchester Circuit of the Methodist Church for allowing me to continue a connection which I have always valued.

*Deo gratias!*

# 1

# LOSING SIGHT OF CHURCH

I AM A UNITED Reformed minister, a dissenter by nature and conviction. My roots are in East Anglia with its wide skies, cold east wind, saltmarsh, and long indented river estuaries like the Blackwater,

> where the coastline doubles up on itself
> as if punched in the gut by the god Meander,
> who likes to dabble in landscapes
> but with this one, lost his grip.[1]

This was the Nonconformist heartland, the local radicalism reinforced by contacts with Dutch Reformed and French Huguenot refugees, of whom my family was one. Church has been part of me all of my life. I was preaching by the time I was sixteen, reading Calvin in spare moments in secondary school and offering for the ministry while in the Sixth Form. Norfolk Congregationalism gave me a critical cast of mind, a dissenter's willingness to be in a minority, and a belief that the local church is what really matters. For nearly forty years it was in such congregations that I invested my life. Today my sympathies are more ecumenical, but church goes deep into who I am.

I trained for the ministry at Mansfield College at Oxford and was ordained at Freemantle United Reformed Church in Southampton in 1975. I thought then the church was in a desperate state, with very few young people, and a real chasm between the modern world and Christian faith. "We're more popular than Jesus now," the Beatle John Lennon told the rock

---

1. Greenlaw, *Minsk*, 11.

journalist Maureen Cleave. "I don't know which will go first—rock 'n' roll or Christianity."[2] Crass though this was, it was not out of tune with the time. Psychedelic flower power was not exactly in tune with church life. The sexual revolution, though not as widespread as people imagined, was real enough to make Christian sexual codes look increasingly archaic. The Hull University librarian and poet Philip Larkin, who lived just along the road from me in Pearson Park, famously wrote:

> Sexual intercourse began
> In nineteen sixty-three....
> Between the end of the "Chatterley" ban
> And the Beatles' first LP[3]

It was nonsense of course but it felt rather like it at the time. An increasingly secular world seemed to have little room for God, and at Hull University I had been to lectures by the young radical theologian Alistair Kee urging us that God was dead.[4]

None of this worried me very much or put me off from ordination. Why should it? Great hopeful movements were around in the church. John Robinson's *Honest to God* had fired me with the conviction that the church could change and be renewed. In his first confirmation address in Southwark, Robinson told the confirmands, "You are coming into active membership of the Church at a time when great things are afoot. I believe that in England we may be at a turning of the tide. Indeed in Cambridge, where I have recently come from, I am convinced that the tide has already turned."[5] A secular gospel would speak to those whom the old religious language did not. There could be what Bonhoeffer called "Religionless Christianity." And the old pattern of a church divided over issues which most modern people cared very little about would be ended as organic union created a church united for mission and service. At the Nottingham Conference initiated by the British Council of Churches in 1964, a commitment was made to seek unity not later than Easter Day 1980. In the Roman Catholic Church, the Second Vatican Council, meeting between October 1962 and December 1965, led not only to a change of the mass from Latin to local languages, but also emphasized that the whole church is

---

2. *Evening Standard*, Mar 4, 1966.
3. Larkin, *Collected Poems*, 167.
4. See Kee, *Way of Transcendence*.
5. James, *Life of Bishop John A. T. Robinson*, 111.

the people of God and seemed to be opening the way to a less hierarchical church. Relations between Catholics and Protestants rapidly began to change. At Hull University it seemed natural to me to lunch at the Catholic Chaplaincy and join in discussions about the ordination of women to the priesthood, which surely could not be far away. When I was ordained, I naively asked the local Catholic priest if he would be among those who laid hands on me in the ordination prayer and had to be reminded that we hadn't got that far yet! In the United States Martin Luther King was demonstrating the social relevance of the gospel in his challenge to racism and militarism. It seemed a glorious time of hope. It helped of course that I was young!

It was not all illusion, but a lot of it was. There was no organic unity, except for the not very significant creation of the United Reformed Church. The most radical commitment, unity by 1980, not only was not achieved but simply never became a priority for most of the churches. The delegates at Nottingham may have voted for unity but the denominations had not and showed limited commitment to the prospect. Theology became more conservative and cautious. There were positives which lasted. A generation of young people inspired by *Honest to God* were to play an important part in church leadership for the next fifty years. Though rarely uniting most churches did draw closer to each other. In the Catholic Church, Vatican Two brought real change and in Merseyside when I ministered there, it was exhilarating to see the Anglican Bishop and the Catholic Archbishop ministering together in a way that shamed the old sectarianism. But there was no New Reformation. Quite soon John Robinson retreated back to Cambridge and it became apparent the tide had not in fact turned even there. Church decline continued and grew infinitely worse. My own United Reformed Church crumbled. If I could go back to the churches which in the 1960s I thought so in decline, and with such elderly congregations, what would strike me now is how many young people there were, and how much larger the congregations than today. When I was ordained at Freemantle its 117 members made it the second smallest URC in Southampton, today that membership would make it twice the size of the largest. Did I really have three elders in their twenties? Did we really have fifty-four children—more than all the remaining Southampton URCs put together have today?

## WHEN CHURCHES FALL COMPLETELY OUT OF USE

The context of my ministry was not to be growth and renewal but a struggle with accelerating decline and fading belief. The sociology of religion has important insights here. Christians often view faith and church life in individual terms. But there is such a thing as social structure—we are part of society, the groups within it have characteristics which don't just break down to individual choices, and their values and attitudes get inside us. This is the principle of synergy which is the theoretical basis of sociology. Without it sociology is hardly possible; with it comes insights which could hardly be more important. This is absolutely fundamental to understanding religion and to the current decline of the churches.

The essential principle here is that belief is not simply an individual matter; what seems likely to us will be insecure unless socially validated. As Peter Berger says,

> The reality of the Christian world depends upon the presence of social structures within which this reality is taken for granted . . . When this plausibility structure loses its intactness or continuity, the Christian world begins to totter and its reality ceases to impose itself as self-evident truth.[6]

This has been the fundamental problem facing Christian belief all my lifetime.

Just to take one example, Arthur Macarthur was the general secretary of the Presbyterian Church of England and a moving force in the creation of the URC, whom I knew because his son was a member of my church in Swindon. Arthur was deeply Presbyterian. He didn't get those beliefs out of thin air. He was a Northumbrian, that part of England where Presbyterianism had really taken root. There you were part of a tightly knit Presbyterian world. His father was session clerk. His mother and his aunt were secretaries of Presbyterian women's organizations. His grandfather was a Presbyterian minister. As he grew up, he was known as the "little elder" and thought it a compliment. He trained for the ministry at Westminster College in Cambridge, in those days a very Presbyterian place. In his autobiography he writes, "I was a Christian and a Presbyterian and took both things as facts of life."[7] With that background it was highly likely he would see it so. But today, as he says, that world has been destroyed

---

6. Berger, *Social Reality*, 55.
7. Macarthur, *Setting Up Signs*, 11.

by the acids of modernity. His grandchildren would grow up in a secular environment which doubted and questioned those beliefs, making them harder to hold. Few people growing up in Northumberland today will become Presbyterian in the way he did. A different time, place, and social context changes the kind of people we become.

The process by which British culture is leaving its Christian past is not going to be reversed any time soon. The sociological term for it is secularization. In a poetic phrase Max Weber, one of the founders of social science, called it the "disenchantment of the world," and it finds classic expression in Britain in Bryan Wilson's *Religion in a Secular Society*. It is not uncontested, and is open to definition and qualification, but it is fundamental to our religious experience, at least in Europe and North America. It has been at the very core of my experience of church life. My whole ministry has been a struggle with decline, trying to keep hopes alive and a rickety boat afloat. In 1500 it was almost axiomatic to interpret the world in Christian terms; today it is countercultural. My choice of sociology as a first degree at Hull was more a function of a limited choice of courses and universities after failing my French O-level examination. After applying I looked up the word "sociology" in the dictionary. But it gave me a social perspective for the study of religion which is absolutely vital. There might have been less talk about "Decades of Evangelism" reversing decline if churches had faced the reality of deep-seated cultural change.

Historically, Christian belief provided the code of conscience and belief of European culture. Now those old certainties had come apart, and to many Christianity seems curious and alien. Churches are sinking beneath the horizon. Drawing on the European Social Survey, the British academic Stephen Bullivant published a concise report, *Europe's Young Adults and Religion*, to assist the deliberations of the Synod of Catholic Bishops and concluded, "Christianity as a default, as a norm, is gone, and probably gone for good—or at least for the next hundred years. . . . The new default setting is 'no religion,' and the few who are religious see themselves as swimming against the tide."[8]

In Philip Larkin's wonderful poem "Church Going," a cyclist who knows only a little about church, enters a deserted building and looks around and asks,

---

8. *Guardian*, Mar 21, 2018.

> When churches will fall completely out of use
> What we shall turn them into.[9]

The prospect may be exaggerated, but the basic situation is unmistakable. The 2021 census showed the number of people who identify as Christian in England and Wales at 46 percent has dropped below half for the first time, while the number who say they have no religion at 37.5 percent has trebled in twenty years.[10] The significance of these exact statistics should not be overestimated. In many cases the involvement with the church of those who identified as Christian was already nominal, often a reflection of the ideological furniture of their early lives rather than implying any active involvement with church or faith. This is not the moment, as some have suggested, when England ceased to a Christian nation—this was certainly much earlier. But the process was intensifying, and for the churches the reality was becoming starker.

Active church membership is in severe decline, and those who are left are often elderly. The latest estimate I have seen is that only about 4.9 percent attend church on a Sunday (prior to lockdown) with the highest percentage of attenders in the 65–74 age range.[11] In the Church of England one survey in 2018 found over 30 percent of attenders were over seventy-five, and only 4 percent under thirty-four.[12] More than a quarter of churches have fewer than twenty worshipers on a Sunday. The decline is most evident among the young. In Victorian England 50 percent of the population attended church, and even those who didn't regularly attend might send their children to Sunday school. By 1850 approximately two million British children attended weekly religious classes.[13] By 2021 there were only 62,000 children attending in the Church of England on a Sunday.[14] As late as 1953 there were 226,500 children and 31,000 teachers in the Congregational Union of England and Wales, and a church like Purley had 668 children.[15] Today the United Reformed Church claims an average of 4,495 children at its services, and Purley has 7 children in worship.[16]

---

9. Larkin, *Collected Poems*, 97
10. *Times*, Nov 29, 2022.
11. Brierley, *UK Church Statistics*, 13.4.
12. Morris, *People's Church*, 379.
13. Laqueur, *Religion and Respectability*, 44.
14. Church of England, *Statistics for Mission 2021*, table 7.
15. *Congregational Yearbook*, 1953.
16. *United Reformed Church Yearbook*, 2021.

This is not simply a British phenomenon—it is true for nearly all of Europe (including formerly Catholic Ireland) and increasingly of the United States. The late Henri Nouwen went back before he died to his boyhood home in the Netherlands, where in one generation Roman Catholicism had lost its place in cultural life. A few months before his death, Nouwen spoke to a paltry crowd of thirty-six students at the seminary he had attended, once bustling with hundreds of eager candidates for priesthood.[17] Today only 7% of self-identified Catholics in Holland attend mass regularly, and half the church buildings have been converted into restaurants, galleries, homes or been destroyed.[18] The church is in deep trouble, maybe in its death throes.

Exactly when this decline began is hard to date with any precision. Was it in the early nineteenth century, or was that a period of growth? Did the Victorians go through a crisis of faith or was it more 'a shiver of anxiety'? It is hard to be sure. We have no adequate numbers for Anglican Easter worshipers or baptisms before 1885, and with the exception of the census of 1851 (the statistics of which are disputable) it is not until the twentieth century that we get regular national surveys of church attendance. Nor will such statistics ever tell us everything—how widely spread and understood were Christian ideas and stories, to what extent were Christian ideas part of education, or literature? Even when they were not deeply committed to the church, quite large numbers of people retained some familiarity with Christian ideas and attended church sporadically.

What we can say with some certainty is that church decline began about 1880 and in the twentieth century, faith became ever more marginal to society. S. J. D. Green in his *The Passing of Protestant England*[19] argues that the long-held link between the English people and the Protestant faith was lost in the period 1920 to 1960. He charts the decline of church attendance, the collapse of the Sunday schools, the abandoning of Sunday observance, and the widening gulf between the churches and the general culture. In this he draws heavily on Rowntree's *English Life and Leisure* which shows a massive reduction in adult attendance at places of worship in York between 1901 and 1948. When increased population is allowed for, attendance had fallen from 35 percent in 1901 to 13 percent in 1948.[20]

---

17. "'Pastoral Council.'"
18. Yancey, "God's Funeral."
19. Green, *Protestant England*.
20. Rowntree and Lavers, *English Life and Leisure*, 342.

Green points to Rowntree's conclusion that "a majority of the population had either explicitly . . . or . . . instinctively rejected so much of the Christian story as related in the New Testament that no church could recognize them as Christian at all."[21]

Whatever the precise details, the general effect is unmistakable. Congregations have mostly declined or closed, and the percentage of the population in real contact with the church has collapsed. Today as a retired minister I still preach most Sundays in the Nonconformist heartland of East Anglia where the reality is often small, mostly elderly congregations, where there may be no one to play the organ and office holders are difficult to replace. It is the closing of great preaching centers of the church like Princes Street Norwich or Warwick Road Coventry or Central Church Bath, with many others certain to follow. It is all the churches where they say to me afterwards, "We don't know how long we can go on." Sunday by Sunday Larkin's phrase "When churches will fall completely out of use" haunts me.

Looking into the future needs to be done with caution. Words of Sam Goldwyn come to mind: "Never prophesy, especially about the future." But a recent analysis by Dr. John Hayward, a mathematician at the University of South Wales, suggested that on current trends the Church in Wales and the United Reformed Church might expect to become extinct by 2038, the Methodist Church and the Church of Scotland by 2040, and the Church of England and the Roman Catholic Church in England by 2062.[22] This almost certainly underestimates the ability of declining organizations to survive, and there are churches which are growing. In London for example there are thriving Catholic congregations among migrant communities and also Pentecostal churches with large black congregations. But for the majority of British people the church is slipping out of sight. My first church in Southampton is currently on the market at £1 million offering: "a great opportunity for property developers."

All sorts of factors have contributed to this collapse including a general loss of institutional commitments. Many organizations from political parties to the St. John's Ambulance brigade find it harder to get people involved. But the problem for churches goes much deeper. Firstly, it is the young especially who are rejecting church. Many young people believe that the church does not represent values which matter to them, such as justice, equality, and inclusivity. Instead, they see the churches as

---

21. Rowntree and Lavers, *English Life and Leisure*, 354–55
22. *Church Times*, May 27, 2022.

representing sexism, homophobia, and hypocrisy. What other conclusion is there when the Church of England has obtained legal exemptions from adhering to British law on matters of equality, including marriage equality? When I speak to my children about matters such as gay rights, to them the whole matter is clear and simple and settled, and the churches' grudging slow acceptance of equal love and equal marriage they find simply incomprehensible. As the Church of England twists and turns offering to bless gay couples but not marry them, it seems to many of the young to be in a moral black hole. To say nothing of bishops who oppose the ordination of women. As Justin Welby admits, "We have to face the fact that the vast majority of people under thirty-five not only think that what we're saying is incomprehensible but also think that we're plain wrong and wicked and equate it to racism and other forms of gross and atrocious injustice. We have to be real about that."[23]

Even more basic is that the language of God no longer speaks to people. When the Irish poet Seamus Heaney was asked what changes he had noticed in a lifetime of writing and reading, he said, "The biggest change in my lifetime has been the evaporation of the transcendent from all our discourse."[24] If we take transcendence to be the recognition of spiritual truth and moral values independent of our choices, related to the deep realities of life itself, the sense that our lives are part of a comprehensive whole, this is now much less true for us. No doubt it is partly the spread of scientific and rational ways of understanding life which often seem self-sufficient—though it is worth noting that 14 percent of those who classify themselves as non-religious believe in the healing power of crystals.[25] Other causes are not hard to find. Significant movements in modern philosophy have argued that religious language is meaningless. A consumer-orientated way of life is not naturally congruent with the spiritual—if there is religious truth, we are often looking the other way and would not be likely to see it. Another Irish poet, Patrick Kavanagh, laments the disenchantment that reigns in a world leached of its sense of wonder, and with it, its intuition for the transcendent.

> We have tasted and tested too much, lover-
> Through a chink too wide there comes in no wonder.[26]

23. *Guardian*, Aug 28, 2013
24. Quoted Jamieson, *Finding the Language of Grace*, 1–2.
25. *Times*, Nov 29, 2022.
26. Kavanagh, *Collected Poems*, 70.

The end result of all this is that religion is not natural to many people, and traditional ideas of God often, and sometimes rightly, seem incredible. Paul Tillich discovered this in the trenches of World War I, Bonhoeffer in Tegel Prison, and I certainly discovered it in my ministry as ideas of God often met blank incomprehension. We often measure secularization by statistics, such as church attendance or church closures but at its heart is something more intangible, how we see our world. The point is well made by Paul Gifford: "In the last few centuries, a new cognitive culture has arisen among western elites, leading to a new way of experiencing reality generally."[27] Compared with our ancestors the world has been desacralized. Where Wordsworth had his hour of "splendour in the grass, of glory in the flower," we are more likely to see only secular realities.

I experienced something of this in Wittenberg, Germany, where Martin Luther launched the Reformation. For a largely secular society our religious past often becomes nostalgic entertainment or sanitized heritage. To me Luther meant justification by faith; to the guides in Martin Luther's house it was the story of a love affair between an ex-monk and an ex-nun. The permanent display that introduces visitors to King's College Chapel in Cambridge begins with the sentence "We exist not only in the world but in an image or picture of the world." Inevitably a largely secular society experiences our religious past in the context of its own images and picture of the world, which make any transcendent meaning harder to find.

A new mindset has arisen. "We don't do God," as Tony Blair's Director of Communications Alistair Campbell put it. Today religious faith seeks to express itself in a culture which has other interests. Theology is dismissed as some curious relic which we have mercifully outgrown. Christians do not find this easy to deal with, either concentrating on understandable secular concerns or simply rehearsing old intellectually discredited dogmatisms. One of the most notable things about the church leadership's response to the COVID crisis was that while many church leaders felt at home talking about the need for food banks, they often found it hard to speak about questions of faith. As *The Times* commented, "In a crisis when its flock requires rather more spiritual succor and sustenance than usual . . . the Church of England has been shockingly absent . . . The Archbishop of Canterbury, the Most Rev. Justin Welby, epitomizes the lackluster response. Since his underwhelming Easter broadcast from his kitchen at Lambeth Palace, our national primate has barely been heard from." To be fair it is

---

27. Gifford, *Plight of Western Religion*, 33.

very hard to speak to the wider society when you are on the edges of the culture with beliefs and presuppositions no longer shared or understood.

Increasingly people simply do not know the Christian story. Asked to decide whether a series of plot lines appeared in the Bible almost half of parents (46 percent) failed to recognize the plot of Noah's Ark as a Bible story; a quarter (27 percent) failed to identify the Bible with the plot of the Good Samaritan. By contrast, over a third thought that storylines featured in *The Hunger Games* (54 percent) and *Harry Potter* (34 percent) were or might be. More than one in four (27 percent) thought the storyline of *Superman* was or could be in the Bible, while (46 percent) thought the same for Dan Brown's novel *The Da Vinci Code*. A survey in the United States found that 12 percent thought that Joan of Arc was Noah's wife, and only one in three could name the four gospels.[28] Steve Bruce puts it starkly: "Most Britons under the age of 60 (that is, those who were not taught its basic ideas at school or Sunday school) have almost no knowledge of Christianity."[29] Sometimes the biblical stories linger in unrecognized secular forms. Just as Jewish or Christian readers enjoying Noah may not recognize the cultural link to Uta-napishti and his ark full of animals in the Babylonian Gilgamesh epic, so Superman fans may not recognize the cultural origins of their story of an otherworldly father who sends his son to earth, where he is raised by human parents and who sacrifices himself to save humanity but is brought back again.[30] Those who imagined a biblical origin for the story were not entirely wrong!

It is with the young that this gulf is most clear. In her British Academy lecture in 2016, Professor Linda Woodhead notes that essentially religious commitment is not being handed on from one generation to the next. The younger you are, the less likely you are to believe and the less likely you are to understand what Christian belief is. "More and more children are being raised in Britain with little or no first-hand knowledge of Christianity. Currently many will still have Christian grandparents, but in a generation or two that will have ceased to be the case."[31]

This is not simply a matter of ideas but practices. For a great many of the young worship is not part of their experience, often they have almost no exposure to it except to some degree in schools where probably many of

---

28. Prothero, S. Los Angeles Times, January 12th, 2005.
29. Bruce, "Late Secularization and Religion as Alien," 14.
28. "Superman As Jesus."
31. Woodhead, "No Religion," 5.

those involved in education do not themselves have the skills, experience, and enthusiasm to make it real. My son went to a comprehensive school in South London where few of the children were openly Christian. One day he came home and recounted with scorn that the RE lesson had involved a trip to a nearby church. "They said, 'that's a pulpit. That's where they give the sermon from.' Whatever did they think it was?" The point of course was that a significant number of the children hardly went inside churches or had any clear idea what went on in a service. Worship, like listening to music, is a practice that has to be learned and today it largely isn't. Any working minister will feel the force of this. You know the huge gap which exists between your world and that in which most people live. Sometimes at baptisms large numbers of people who rarely cross church doors find themselves at a service. They don't sing the hymns, often not opening the hymn books; they talk among themselves during the Eucharist; and sometimes when we announce, "the children will now go to their own lessons," they take the opportunity to get out too. Matters are not helped when they are told that the responses are on page four of the blue book, column B.

One measure of this loss can be seen in the ways hymns are no longer part of communal culture. "Abide with Me" may linger at Cup Finals but the words, even when sung, have lost their religious significance. Max Boyce makes the point for the practice of hymn singing at Welsh Rugby matches where "Cwm Rhondda " and "Delilah" have equally little meaning.

Even when people were singing, the words of one had no more meaning than the other.[32] In any meaningful sense religion has been marginalized in British society and its meaning and practices alien in a secular world.

For churches this brutal reality is difficult to take. In his first statement as Archbishop designate Justin Welby felt confidently able to say, "we are at one of those rare points where the tide of events is turning, . . . I feel a massive sense of privilege at being one of those responsible for the leadership of the church in a time of spiritual hunger."[33] Such claims are made often and so far, have always proved a triumph of optimism over reality. Today even evangelical and charismatic churches, which have until recently been growing, are showing signs of decline with the only really

---

32. See Cleaves, "Hymns and Arias."
33. *Guardian*, Nov 9, 2012.

growing churches mostly linked to immigration. Even the Baptist Union has had a 51 percent reduction in its membership between 1970 and 2020.[34]

A huge gulf has opened up between the world of the church and that of the general community. As A. N. Wilson shrewdly observes, "Those millions who polish the car on Sunday mornings and never go to church have bred up two generations of children who probably have only the haziest sense of what the church is."[35] Churches are still prominent in our towns, and even more in our villages. Architecturally they may be appreciated, possibly new uses can be found for them as community space, but their essential meaning slips out of view. As Philip Larkin wrote,

> A shape less recognisable each week,
> A purpose more obscure.[36]

The question is what, if anything, comes next? For a good many people absolutely nothing comes next—it's over. For others the solution is to accept the premise that God talk is obsolete and seek to refashion Christianity without it, with God now simply a linguistic device, a way of describing our own values. This is the Don Cupitt option, and quite a few find it attractive, but nearly all originally grew up in a more traditional Christian faith on which it is clearly parasitic. For others the solution is to shut out the questions and just go believing in the old way—essentially the fundamentalist option. Rather desperately others seek a way out through secular inspired management techniques, endless rebranding, strategizing, PR exercises, and reputational-management. The end results from this are unsurprisingly negligible. As Steve Bruce has argued, because the shared stock of religious knowledge is so limited, the public reputation of the church so low, and church members are mainly so old or drawn from immigrant communities, any imminent revival of religion is unlikely.[37]

I remain deeply committed to the church, critical of it, but still to be found within it. The advent of the COVID virus meant the longest stretch away from church in my life. "Be honest. Do you really miss it?" asked a minister friend, who himself stopped going to church some time ago. I did and I missed even more the chance of trying week in week out to make sense of what the faith means and why church matters. That's my brief here

---

34. Field, *Counting Religion in Britain*, 344–46.
35. Wilson, *Faber Book of Church*, X.
36. Larkin, *Collected Poems*, 98.
37. Bruce, *British Gods*, 252–71.

too. What follows is an attempt to explain what church is and why human life is poorer without it.

## TELL ALL THE TRUTH BUT TELL IT SLANT

I will attempt to be as honest as I can. Of course, try as we may, none of us are totally objective. As a liberal Reformed Christian, I have a particular vantage point which inevitably influences my experience and how I interpret it. What follows is very much from a personal perspective. I am not an academic theologian, and my experience as a teacher was in sociology, not theology. I spent all my ministry in local congregations and never really wished to do anything else. All this gives me a particular, and inevitably rather limited, viewpoint. I am a booky person and quote them rather too much! I love poetry, although I am aware that not everyone shares this particular passion.

My vantage point is resolutely ecumenical. Of my four churches, two were joint URC/Methodist Churches, one of which was in a local ecumenical partnership with Anglican and Baptist churches, the other in a local covenant with Catholic, Quaker, and both an evangelical and a High Church Anglican church. Interestingly the two Anglican churches both seemed to think they had more in common with us than with each other. Another of my churches, though purely URC, was in a LEP with Anglican and Methodist churches. My links with Methodism were particularly strong. I have been to more Methodist meetings than I care to remember and have twice been an acting superintendent minister. At Oxford I was a member of the John Wesley Society and since I retired, have tried to keep up my links with Methodism, even offering to attend the Methodist staff meeting which some might think was going above and beyond the call of duty! I sometimes say that I could probably pass for a Methodist in a bad light. Of the theologians and preachers who most influenced me one was a Baptist, two Presbyterians, one a Lutheran, one a Methodist and one an Anglican. Though I value my particular church, it has no special relationship with the truth. Indeed, it was never my wish to be ordained a United Reformed Church minister. I wanted to minister within a united church. When the United Reformed Church celebrated its fiftieth anniversary I stayed away from the celebrations since the whole point of the church for me was that it was simply to be a staging post to a wider union. I am unambiguously committed to a vision of the one great church whose disunity contradicts its nature and purpose. None the less for all that I speak out of my experience as a United Reformed Church minister.

Equally I am unambiguously a liberal Christian. I happily acknowledge evangelical elements in my theology and am always delighted when an evangelical recognizes them. There's a Christ-centered passion and seriousness about evangelicalism which often puts liberals to shame. But unlike some liberals I never even passed through a fundamentalist phase. It was obvious to me, right back to the time I did my RE A-level in the school chapel side room, that when you put the text of the first three Gospels side by side you found events were often in a different order and differently interpreted. Such things could hardly be ignored. I know very well that liberal Christianity comes with a health warning. It wasn't always as open as it thought it was. It was slow to take women's, black, or gay issues seriously. Adapting to contemporary culture too often meant an uncritical adoption of it. Some aspects of the history of liberal Protestantism are extremely painful to recount. But liberal Christianity is also a hugely rich tradition. It sees intellectual critically as part of faith, knows faith is an open journey not a route to a prescribed destination. It knows infallible guides are all self-delusion. It spurred on biblical scholarship, social justice, ecumenism, and interfaith dialogue. All of that is part of who I am and, I dare to believe, part of the gospel too. As with my URC background it helped me become who I am and shapes what I see.

I am a Reformed, ecumenical, liberal Christian with a perspective on the gospel. Which is to say I have a point of view. This is inevitable. The best any of us can manage is a partial insight from a particular viewpoint—an angle of entry, a slant on truth, simply one perspective among many. I don't for a moment imagine this is the only way you can see things, or how I would necessarily see them if my background was different. The best any of us can do is what Emily Dickinson advises: "Tell all the truth but tell it slant."[38]

My objective as the church slips out of sight is to explain my belief in it as honestly as I can. Losing touch with church has meant a break with the western cultural past, its history, its music, its art, its literature, much of which cannot fully be understood without its religious heritage. But more importantly the church is part of the way the Jesus tradition is lived out in the world. Within it, community is experienced, values nurtured, God's presence in the world is embodied in a people. Jesus intended it; God's love

---

38. Dickinson, *Complete Poems*, 506–67.

is proclaimed and, at least sometimes, lived out within it; and the value and dignity of the human as made in the image of God is explored. Take it away and something special has gone. Barbara Wheeler says we have crossed a cultural divide. Before, if you didn't hold traditional religious beliefs and belong to a church you felt obliged to explain yourself. Now the pressure is to explain why you do.[39] This is my answer.

---

39. Wheeler, *Who Needs the Church*.

# 2

# A VERY HUMAN INSTITUTION

THERE IS A CATHOLIC joke that parodies the story in John 8 where Jesus reaches out to the woman taken in adultery. The joke follows the Gospel story to the point where Jesus says, "Let any among you who is without sin be the first to throw a stone at her" (John 8:7). The crowd begin to drop their stones and leave, but then suddenly someone throws a large brick, which hits the woman on the head and knocks her to the ground. "Who threw that?" demands Jesus. No one owns up. Jesus surveys the crowd and sees a small sheepish face at the back. He sighs and says, "Mother, please go home." The story is not really about Mary but us. Whatever we believe about Mary none of us are perfect and should never imagine we are for one moment. Certainly, the Church isn't.

I believe in the Church. It originated from the ministry of Jesus and is where the news of God's love in Jesus Christ is proclaimed and believed. I have had the privilege of serving as minister of four local congregations and have seen the difference the Church can make in people's lives. In many different ways, most of them undramatic, quiet, and inconspicuous, they have demonstrated what the love of God looks like. I am grateful my ministry has been in the United Reformed Church which gave me a freedom to be myself, which I hugely valued. My purpose is to make as clearly as I can the case for the church. But to do this I have to be honest and not to pretend that the church is better than it is. So, I want to face the negative first. To be frank I do not find this easy to write, and possibly some may not find it easy to read. But the truth is not optional.

## A SERIOUS HOUSE

In all honesty the church is a very peculiar institution. It is called the *holy* Catholic Church, and many claim either that it possesses an infallible book or that the pronouncements of its leader are infallible. Church leaders can be addressed as "Your Holiness" or "Your Beatitude." It often speaks of its moral role in society. From this one might infer that the church is in some way qualitatively different from any other institution and its office holders exemplars of human conduct. Any such assumption would be mistaken. The church is a human institution, capable of good things but often deeply flawed morally and with only an ambiguous relationship to the purposes it purports to serve. This should surprise no one. All institutions overclaim for themselves and in practice become more concerned with their own survival than their original purpose. People within them pursue their own career strategies. This is absolutely true of the church. Church bureaucracies are just as likely as any other to become introverted, to attempt to control committees and manipulate agendas. Church leaders often seek what are seen as "better posts," want to ensure their jobs are secure, and seek to protect their reputations even at the cost of truth. Church magazines cannot be relied upon to tell the truth about what goes on within them. They after all have a product to promote. As for theology and preaching, these are inevitably enmeshed within culture, often with self-interested and local motivations. It should surprise no one that the patriarch of the Russian Orthodox Church supports the Russian invasion of Ukraine, and the patriarch of the Ukrainian Orthodox Church does not. Nationalism can warp faith, with demonstrators storming the Capital building shouting, "God, Guns, and Trump." Preachers habitually choose their words carefully in order to please, or at least not to alienate, their congregations or church hierarchies. It is far from unknown for theologians to be intellectually uncommitted to truth.

None of this is a new discovery. During a church schism in which the three different factions each had their own pope, when the self-styled John XXIII was deposed in 1415, Gibbon dryly recounts that, "The more scandalous charges were suppressed; the vicar of Christ was accused only of piracy, rape, sodomy, murder and incest."[1] No one who knows church history should be in any doubt as to the moral ambiguity of the church. From the very beginning the churches we see in the New Testament suffer

---

1. Gibbon, *History of the Decline*, 241. Historical note: The original Pope John XXIII was later no longer recognized, leaving this title free for reuse by the better-known twentieth-century pope.

from factional disagreement, social tensions, and personal moral failure. Most spectacularly in Corinth, there was class-based hostility, drunkenness at communion, litigation between members of the church, involvement with prostitutes, and "sexual immorality . . . of a kind not found even among pagans" (1 Cor 5:1). The author of Revelation calls Ephesus a loveless church (Rev 2:4). The evolving church had a fine record of concern for the poor but could also be deeply intolerant. The persecution of Jesus' own Jewish people is to the eternal shame of Christianity, and as far as we can estimate more Christians were killed by their fellow Christians after the conversion of Constantine than had died before at the hands of the Romans.[2] Nor was book burning a Nazi invention.

The church finds this hard to acknowledge; it does not fit with its self-image or its self-promotion. To be fair it is sometimes hard to criticize what you love. Too often we allow the dream to obscure the reality. We prefer Luther bravely speaking out for the truth to Luther the vicious antisemite. We prefer not to see the flaws in Mother Theresa, who all her life hid her real feelings. We prefer a mythologized story of Bonhoeffer the martyr to the reality of the failure of the German Church. Gary Dorrien puts this brutally: "Bonhoeffer is famous mostly for being the person who helps Christians feel better about the craven Christian cowardice and evil of the Nazi period."[3] We prefer not to dwell on the fact that one thing Tillich, Martin Luther King, and Barth all had in common was adultery. The inconvenient truth is that the church is radically flawed in a way its rhetoric does not acknowledge.

Recently nothing has revealed the flawed nature of the Church more starkly than the sexual abuse scandals which have so damaged the moral authority of the church. This has been a moral catastrophe. The sheer scale and shocking nature of the survivors' accounts discovered for example by the government established Independent Inquiry into Child Sexual Abuse (IICSA) in England and Wales were truly horrendous. It found that between the 1940s and 2018, 390 clergy members or people in positions of trust were convicted of child sex offences, but this is almost certainly only the tip of the iceberg. In Ireland since 2002, multiple reports and investigations have shed light on nearly 15,000 cases of sexual abuse committed between 1970 and 1990. What has been most morally offensive about the recent child abuse scandals is not just that some clergy were sexual predators but

---

2. MacMullen, *Changes in the Roman Empire*, 156, 267.
3. Dorrien, "Theological and the Political."

how often hierarchies were more concerned to protect the institution and the perpetrators rather than the victims. As one Irish survivor dramatically but fairly put it:

> You know, you only have to do a few Google searches to see loads of examples of popes and bishops saying, 'We didn't know.' Like the rest of society, we didn't understand such things were possible. They did. They lied.[4]

In England the IICSA report into the elite Catholic boarding schools at Ampleforth and Downside found that "Safeguarding children was less important than the reputation of the Church and the wellbeing of the abusive monks. Even after new procedures were introduced in 2001, when monks gave the appearance of co-operation and trust, their approach could be summarized as a 'tell them nothing' attitude."[5]

The damage this has done to the moral authority of the churches is immense and in Ireland, for example, has been a major factor in the rapid secularization of Irish society. To begin with I really did know virtually nothing about any of this. Sexual abuse, or the procedures to adopt when it occurred, was never mentioned in my theological training. When twenty years into ministry someone first disclosed to me that they had been sexually abused I was quite out of my depth and of very little use. In one of my churches, after I left, one of the children told his parents that one of the leaders of a youth organization had behaved inappropriately at camp. They didn't fully believe him, because surely they would not do this kind of thing? Sadly, bit by bit, the enormity of it all became clearer. Part of the learning experience for me came with pastoral involvement with a URC minister who used his position to take sexual advantage of vulnerable women. His congregation thought this could be covered by Christian forgiveness. I came to realize that, even when there were not gross cover ups, churches liked to keep things as quiet as possible, perhaps to protect the innocent but certainly to protect their reputation. When one URC minister was convicted of sexually abusing children, pressure was unsuccessfully put on the URC monthly magazine, *Reform*, not to include any reference to him. Church culture did begin to change. Safeguarding became a standard part of church life. I was never quite sure how directly effective it was, but it certainly raised awareness. Ministry was now less innocent. I decided that

4. Euronews, "Sins of the Fathers."
5. *Sunday Times*, Sep 2, 2018.

if a young person was alone in the house when I called, I should not go in, and I became very circumspect about putting my arms around people who were upset. In one of my churches, allegations were brought against a youth work leader who made the mistake of reading the riot act to someone he believed guilty of bullying in a one-to-one meeting. In the circumstances it was, in the nature of things, hard to prove what might or might not have happened. It brought in the police (who took no action) but cost the church a youth leader and a youth group.

The truth is that abuse, and cover-ups, have been widespread. It is not just Catholics and Anglo-Catholics. There have been several cases of URC ministers, some of them prominent within the denomination, who were found guilty of sexual abuse of children and/or adults, one of whom was described by the judge as a monster. An internal URC report found instances where allegations of abuse had been dismissed out of hand and occasions where the church had failed to refer them to statutory agencies or take the appropriate follow-up action. "There is evidence that children tried to share their stories, but these were not acted upon or believed at the time of disclosure."[6]

Perpetrators came from all kinds of theological backgrounds. Liberal Christians who violated moral boundaries, charismatic pastors having secret "wrestling matches" with young men, or authoritarian evangelicals giving naked beatings to vulnerable adults. When a former Bishop, Peter Ball was jailed for indecent assault, the official report in the Church of England concluded, "The Church colluded with that rather than seeking to help those he had harmed or assuring itself of the safety of others."[7] IICSA concluded, "The culture of the Church of England facilitated it becoming a place where abusers could hide."[8] In the Methodist Church an internal report found that the church was "not seen as a safe place" by many female members because of a "misogynistic and toxic" attitude towards women. It criticized senior leaders' "failure to respond" to allegations of abusive and discriminatory behavior, which created a "difficult environment" for women in the church.[9] In total, it identified 1,885 cases with reported abuse including alleged sexual, physical, emotional and domestic abuse, as well as cases of neglect. One of the abuse survivors who responded to the survey

6. *Christian Today*, Nov 23 2018.
7. "Church 'Colluded' with Sex Abuse Bishop."
8. *Independent*, Oct 6, 2020.
9. *Times*, May 22, 2023.

said, "I have learnt that it is impossible to recover from sexual abuse when no-one recognizes the seriousness of it. My Church did not want a scandal, my parents did not want a scandal. I was left to feel worthless and devalued, while the man was left to get on with his life and for all I know to repeat the crime with someone else."[10]

The effect of this scandal on the moral authority of the church has been considerable and devastating. Church culture has begun to change. Disciplinary procedures were tightened. A former archbishop of Canterbury was suspended for a time in an abuse inquiry. A former archbishop of York was suspended from active ministry in the diocese of Newcastle after he rejected the finding of a church safeguarding review, that he had failed to act on a non-recent disclosure of abuse. Equally the Methodist Church has been willing to ban one past Methodist president of conference for life from any role as a Methodist minister and suspend the immediate ex-vice president following allegations of inappropriate behavior (hotly denied). Another ex-president was also suspended following a complaint that he failed to deal appropriately with a complaint about a third party. This is a sign of changing times, though a sobering one in the seniority of those accused.

Today there is real remorse and dismay. So there should be. But I am not sure even now that those who are abused would be wise always to trust the church. New cases are still coming to light. I note the comment of Julie Conalty, the bishop of Birkenhead and the church's own deputy lead for safeguarding, on the sacking of the Church's safeguarding body in 2023:

> Today the church is less accountable. To remove, at short notice, the strongest independent voices holding the CofE to account for its safeguarding failings makes us look resistant to robust scrutiny and challenge—which, of course, we are.[11]

In any case, that abuse and cover-ups should have been so widespread and involved so many figures in so many churches is a deep shame and salutary to anyone who sees the Church as part of God's intention. "Lilies that fester, smell far worse than weeds."[12]

No one should imagine this particularly dramatic moral catastrophe is simply a one-off. Greed, for example, has also been a constant feature of

---

10. *Guardian*, May 28, 2023
11. *Daily Telegraph*, Jun 22, 2023.
12. Shakespeare, *Complete Works*, 1083.

church life. In the fourteenth century, in his *The Pardoner's Tale*, Geoffrey Chaucer gives a picture of a corrupt seller of dubious relics who is greedily swindling people. Anyone who wants to see greed at its most extreme today need do no more than look at the most important bureaucracy in the Christian church, the Vatican. This has been riddled with corruption, financial, sexual, and sometimes even criminal.[13] A 487-page indictment drawn up by the church accused Cardinal Becciu of embezzlement, money laundering, fraud, extortion, and abuse of office. It "sheds light on hefty bank transfers, text messages between collaborators from seized cell phones—even bags of money changing hands and secret meetings in luxury hotels."[14] Again the problem is ecumenical as witnessed by the weary round of TV evangelists whose guiding principle seems to be that counting the offerings—it is "one for Jesus, one for me." A good many charismatic pastors see the church as an opportunity to get rich. John Milton referred in his time to those

> Who all the sacred mysteries of Heaven
> To their own vile advantages shall turn
> Of lucre and ambition.[15]

The simple fact is that the line between good and evil does not lie at the church door. There is great goodness outside and no shortage of utter scoundrels within. In an insightful moment, the book of Genesis, after humanity's expulsion from Eden, indicates that an angel with a flaming sword now stands on guard to prevent our return.[16] Crossing the church door does not invalidate that. All this I know and share in.

My experience of this has been rather limited—no one offers bags of money to United Reformed Church ministers. But it does include seeing one church's collections dramatically rise when the person counting the offerings retired! I have known an alarming number of clergy who had extramarital affairs. I was involved when a member of the United Reformed Church was sentenced for death threats against a gay member of a local church, and an attempt made locally to cover it up. I've had to ban someone from church because their actions were making women members of the congregation uneasy. I've been happy in all the churches I've ministered

---

13. See Martel, *In the Closet of the Vatican.*
14. *Daily Mail*, Jul 25, 2022.
15. Milton, *Poetical Works*, 456.
16. Gen 3:24.

to, but all had their difficulties. They can breed conflict over absolute trivia or questions of no religious significance. When I arrived as minister at Immanuel Swindon there was heated contention about the resurfacing of the car park—a matter in which I was able with total honesty to adopt a policy of ignorance-based neutrality. Since over thirty years later the car park has not been resurfaced again, I assume they made the right decision.

The church is a human institution full of flawed people, sometimes with good intentions, sometimes capable of great goodness, but often mediocre or worse. Churches find this very difficult to accept because it so totally contradicts their self-image and their rhetoric. As Stephen Parsons says, "The fantasy perfect church and infallible leaders are what they pine after, and so they create that reality in their minds, even if it does not in fact exist."[17] All this is a matter for shame, but not necessarily surprise. Life is so complex and contradictory; it has such heights and such depths, that good and evil are never wholly separate. Reinhold Niebuhr once observed the doctrine of original sin is the only empirically verifiable doctrine of Christian faith.[18] Human moral fragility is found in every area of life. Oxfam workers exploit poor women, MPs exploit their expenses, political parties talk of fraternity but loathe their fellow party members, police commit crime, cricket clubs racially discriminate, United Nations agencies become financially corrupt. The common factor in human evil is not religion but humanity. Alexander Solzhenitsyn saw it in a Soviet labor camp. The desperate struggle for life revealed things as they really were. Reflecting on it he said, "Gradually it was disclosed to me that the line separating good and evil passes, not between states, not between classes, not between political parties either, but right through every human heart—and through all human hearts."[19] In human life there is simply no alternative to working with lives that fall short of what we hope and institutions that are often self-serving.

What is imperative is never to gloss over the church's moral failures but to be resolutely self-critical. Karl Marx once said that all criticism begins with the criticism of religion. I would like to rephrase that—all good religion begins with the criticism of religion. "Judgement must begin at the house of God" (1 Pet 4:17). As Karl Barth put it, "Historic Christianity itself is a religion, and must constantly come under the criticism of the

17. Parsons, "When a Church Fails to Care."
18. Niebuhr, *Man's Nature and His Communities*, 24.
19. Solzhenitsyn, *Gulag Archipelago*, 615.

gospel."[20] Which is why, of all people, Christians should be most critical of the church. If I am going to make a case for the church, it has to be done with both realism and honesty. The question is not, Are churches uniquely of all human institutions, perfect? It is, are there times, moments, and occasions, when grace is found and the kingdom glimpsed through it? My case is that there are. I know the church too well to take its pretensions seriously, but I have seen enough goodness and caught sight of too many visions to make me cynical. Church is where I was formed as a person, and where some of the great experiences in my life have come, and where my hopes have been grounded. It is where ordinary people come together in search of something greater than themselves and find it in the Christian story. Sometimes at least churches can be communities of love, inclusion, and justice. R. S. Thomas offers a wonderful picture:

> It's a long way off but inside it
> There are quite different things going on:
> Festivals at which the poor man
> Is king and the consumptive is
> Healed; mirrors in which the blind look
> At themselves and love looks at them.[21]

Church is "a serious house, on serious earth,"[22] where, as Langdon Gilkey says, "finitude, fate, sin and death are articulated, confessed and resolved through grace."[23] It is out of this that my case will be made.

---

20. Barth, *Church Dogmatics*, 50
21. Thomas, *Collected Poems*, 233.
22. Larkin, *Collected Poems*, 97.
23. Gilkey, *American Congregations*, 108.

# 3

# SACRED SPACE—A SYMPHONY IN STONE

THE QUESTION IS, WHERE to start? There is a case for starting with Jesus since Christian faith centers on his story. There is a case for starting with the people since they are the real meaning of church. But I have decided to start with buildings, since this is the most obvious sign of church and is what Larkin's cyclist is drawn by. In the UK there are something like 40,000 buildings used for religious worship. Some are functional, some are ugly, some evoke wonder like the Gothic churches where, as Chesterton said,

> Giants lift up their heads to wonder
> How high the hands of man could go.[1]

There they are, unmistakable evidence of Christian history and Christian presence. The motives of those who built them were mixed. Sometimes it may have had more to do with civic, personal, or ecclesiastical pride than any concern for the transcendent. With commendable honesty when Christ Church URC Port Sunlight celebrates its Founder's Day, it is William Hulme Lever, First Viscount Leverhulme, whom they have in mind. Today some are largely given over to tourists. But they also can be sacred space. At the heart of religion is the experience of the sacred, the looking beyond ourselves, to what Rudolf Otto called the *mysterium tremendum et fascinans*,[2] the numinous, transcendent, the holy. This can be experienced anywhere, in any place at any time, but to an extent that no

---

1. Chesterton, *Ballad of St. Barbara*, 63.
2. Otto, *Idea of the Holy*, 26–27.

other building does, church buildings can be sacred spaces, places which mediate the experiences to which they witness, mysticism in stone and glass. Sometimes they make God real.

The capacity of certain places to evoke the sense of something more than the ordinary goes deep into our past. When I was in Swindon I came to know and love the Ridgeway, which is one of England's most ancient tracks. People have been walking it for 5000 years, along the way from Avebury to Ivinghoe Beacon. If you walk it near Uffington, you can see the oldest white horse in Britain, probably from the Bronze Age. Near it is Uffington Castle, an iron age hill fort, and Dragon Hill where, according to the legend, St. George slew the dragon. Go on a little further and you come to Wayland's Smithy, which has been sacred space for 5000 years. Here a barrow for the bodies of fourteen people was constructed between 3590 BC and 3550 BC, and a little later a far larger barrow was constructed on top. It is one of the most atmospheric places I know. I never feel quite at ease there; there is something strange, almost eery, certainly something beyond the ordinary. You understand why it has been a place of worship for so long and why there are always votive offerings still there today. It is not a secular place.

Throughout history people have been drawn to graves, caves, stone circles, rivers, springs, clumps of trees, mountains, headlands overlooking the sea. Biblically it is Moses being told to take his shoes off because he was standing on holy ground or the disciples grasping who Jesus is on the Mount of Transfiguration. When Christians came to build places of worship, they sought to catch wonder in stone. They can be what is known in Celtic Christian spirituality as "thin places," places in our lives and in our world where there is only a very thin veil, gossamer thin, separating heaven from earth. Sharlande Sledge gives this description:

> 'Thin places,' the Celts call this space,
> Both seen and unseen,
> Where the door between the world
> And the next is cracked open for a moment
> And the light is not all on the other side.[3]

Pilgrimages to sacred places are important to many religious traditions. It might be to Rome or Jerusalem or the five-hundred-mile walk along the Camino de Santiago to the shrine of St. James, or in England a visit to the Holy Land of Walsingham, or along St. Cuthbert's Way. Chaucer began his

---

3. Sledge, "Thin Places," unpublished poem.

celebrated pilgrimage narrative by reminding us of the soul's longing for such transformative journeys:

> Then people think of holy pilgrimages,
> Pilgrims dream of setting foot on far-off
> Lands, or worship at distant shrines, their thoughts
> Reaching for grace.[4]

Today for many people Iona is like this. Laura Béres describes three visits to the abbey. Her fellow pilgrims found their spiritual awareness deepened both by the place and the experience of community. One of her interviewees reported that "each time she came to Iona she was able to listen to God better and learn through the constantly changing physical scene around her."[5] She felt it too:

> Iona felt like home. It felt as though the saints and angels were walking with me . . . I felt completely safe. And here, back in Glasgow with the Orange parade going on, it feels as though there is a thickness . . . a buffer of distraction and human failing, with layers and layers of stuff and junk, a feeling of thickness rather than thinness.[6]

For many it is Gothic architecture which does this most dramatically. Soaring upwards, full of color and light, it brings an overwhelming experience of beauty and, it believes, of truth. On the doors of the first great Gothic Church, St. Denys in Paris, its patron Abbot Suger put the words, "The dull mind rises to the truth through material things." The point is fundamental. Religious truth can come from what we see and touch. Go to St. Denys or Salisbury or Lincoln Cathedrals, and you may catch a glimpse of the harmony of heaven. In D. H. Lawrence's *The Rainbow*, Will Brangwen is overwhelmed by Lincoln Cathedral:

> His soul leapt, soared up into the great church. His body stood still, absorbed by the height. His soul leapt up into the gloom, into possession, it reeled, it swooned with a great escape, it quivered in the womb. . . Here the stone leapt up from the plain of earth.[7]

---

4. Chaucer, *Canterbury Tales*, Prologue, 11–18.
5. Béres, "Thin Place," 399.
6. Béres, "Thin Place," 400.
7. Lawrence, *Rainbow*, 201.

Often art, which could be rustic or more refined, added to the experience. The interior of the church acted as what was called a *biblia pauperum*, a bible for the poor, and wall paintings, icons, stained glass carvings, and paintings were full of the meaning of faith. Ellen Davis notes that in the Old Testament, the only buildings that receive extended, detailed descriptions are the tabernacle and the temple, communal places of worship. She concludes:

> A sanctuary has a kind of creative capacity of its own. . . . The sanctuary itself deepens religious experience and insight. The physical space that we inhabit as worshippers may itself contribute to our awareness of new possibilities for living in the presence of and to the glory of God.[8]

## HOW I CHANGED MY MIND

Originally sacred space was not part of my tradition. Calvin would have none of it. Churches were not sacred places; they were places where one went with others to hear the Word of God. In the week they would often be locked, you could after all pray to God anywhere at any time. In any case East Anglian Nonconformity had its grand churches in the larger towns, but my experience of it was of a rather cramped world of modest red brick and sometimes quite ugly buildings. The façade of Harleston Congregational Church, where I first came into church membership, was not unimpressive, justifying Pevsner's description of it as "surprisingly large and townish," but inside the effect of the galleries and pews to a child was heavy and gloomy. Dickens could be merciless towards dissenting chapels. "It was a little Bethel, a Bethel of the smallest dimensions, with a small number of small pews, and a small pulpit in which a small gentleman . . . was delivering in a by no means small voice, a by no means small sermon."[9] Harleston was more than that. The sermons were not long, and the minister did not shout. But as a child it did seem a small world, and the building left me unmoved. It was a place with pulpit and organ—nothing more.

Then came Oxford. Despite the traffic jams and crocodiles of tourists, Oxford thrilled me with its sheer beauty. I was one with W. B. Yeats: "I wonder anybody does anything at Oxford but dream and remember, the

---

8. Davis, "Wise and Holy Work," 6.
9. Dickens, *Old Curiosity Shop*.

place is so beautiful."[10] I was at Mansfield College with its wonderful light Basil Champneys neo-Gothic. Its chapel, with its stained-glass windows of the saints and statues of the great Reformers, has been described as the most Catholic place in Oxford. Horton Davies called it "perhaps the finest example of Free Church neo-Gothic building"[11] and David Cornick, "a bold fugue in stained glass, statues and wood."[12] Here the building itself moved me to worship—a quite new experience. The sermon might be dull, but there could still be a wonder in the organ voluntary, or the sense of space, or the light through the stained glass.

It is not that church buildings have some unique quality. The beauty of the chapel was of a kind with the experience of the amazing dome of the Radcliffe Camera against the night sky, or walking in Christ Church Meadow. But at Mansfield Gothic architecture explicitly joined with stained glass and organ to contextualize the experience in religious wonder.

> And we, the marvel seeing,
> Forget our selfish being,
> For joy of beauty not our own.[13]

Then came Riverside. When in Oxford and struggling with what in any positive sense faith might mean, I had been profoundly influenced by a book of Harry Emerson Fosdick's sermons I found in a second-hand bookshop. Visiting New York, I made a point of worshiping at Riverside Church, built for Fosdick after fundamentalists ended his ministry at New York's First Presbyterian Church. I was not prepared for what I found. Riverside was built for preaching but also in the conviction, as Fosdick put it, that "beauty is a roadway to God."[14] Standing beside the Hudson River, with the nave modelled on Chartres Cathedral, Riverside has the tallest church tower in America, the largest carillon of bells in the world, and dramatic stained glass. As the seemingly endless procession of choir and clergy entered for the processional hymn the tears ran down my face. I still vaguely remember the sermon, but that was not what moved me. It was the power of sacred space, the way that beauty can give us a sense of the sublime and make us feel part of something bigger than ourselves, a reality

10. Yeats, *Collected Letters*.
11. Davies, *From Newman to Martineau*, 56.
12. Cornick, *Under God's Good Hand*, 122.
13. United Reformed Church, *Rejoice and Sing*, No 51.
14. Miller, *Harry Emerson Fosdick*, 229.

that transcends the everyday and can bring heaven down to earth. Though I didn't know it at the time, this was an idea which was central to the Orthodox tradition of worship. As Germanos, patriarch of Constantinople between 715 and 730, put it, "the church is the earthly heaven in which the heavenly God dwells and moves,"[15] the beauty of the church opens to us something of the wonder of heaven. Nothing at Harleston Congregational had prepared me for this.

## WHAT THE PURITANS MISSED

The Puritans had a point. There is an utterly proper Puritan protest against the way the means becomes the end. The church is not primarily a building but a community. Worship can be valid in any building or none. All this is important. But it was dualistic—seeing God in the word but not in the physical, the artistic, and the ascetic. Edwin Muir saw the point here. In *The Incarnate One*, Muir writes, "The Word made flesh is here made word again."[16] God is found too in beauty, music, and in the sacraments. By losing the idea of sacred space, seeing transcendence as only conveyed by the Word, the more austere Puritanism offered a truncated view of God. There were fine dissenting churches like the Congregational Old Meeting House in Norwich, with its Tuscan and Ionic columns, or the Presbyterian (now Unitarian) Octagon Chapel with its English neo-Palladian architecture which John Wesley called the "finest meeting house in Europe." There were small harmonious chapels like Walpole Old Chapel in Suffolk which, as Christopher Wakeling puts it, has "a kind of hallowed liveliness,"[17] or the charming Quaker house at Jordans (Buckinghamshire), built in 1688. But too often the result of the Reformation was that churches were seen as purely functional, aiming simply to provide an auditorium in which the maximum number of people can clearly hear the preaching.

When in 1819 W. F. Pocock produced the first English pattern book for churches he declared, "the principal point for consideration is the most convenient method of seating the greatest number of persons, to hear distinctively the voice of the reader and preacher."[18] It was a mundane and diminished view—paralleled by a negativity towards church music—another

15. Quoted in Harries, *Beauty and the Horror*, 73.
16. Muir, Collected Poems, 22.
17. Wakeling, *Chapels of England*, 33.
18. Pocock, *Designs for Churches*, 9.

suspiciously Catholic danger. In England the Puritans insisted that such singing should be unaccompanied, often destroying the organs which they regarded as relics of past superstition. During the Civil War, at St. James Nayland in Essex, the Parliamentary forces broke down thirty "superstitious pictures" (probably including stained glass windows) and took down the cross from the steeple. To them it was not vandalism but religious principle. All the color of the medieval church was whitewashed away.

It could not, and mostly did not, last. We are not desiccated calculating machines; we respond to the physical and the spiritual as well as to the intellectual. Something intrinsic to worship had been lost. Not far from me on the Suffolk-Essex border is the Church of St. Stephen Bures, founded by Archbishop Langton in 1218, who believed this to be the spot where St. Edmund was crowned King of Anglia in 855. It is up a farm track, timber roofed, amid trees and looking out over the valley of the Stour. Inside are three tombs for the de Veres, earls of Oxford, including Richard de Vere, who fought at Agincourt, there with his wife Alice, their hands raised in prayer. Simon Jenkins says, "They are tombs of the sort we might expect in Warwick or Westminster, not lost on a Suffolk hillside . . . Yet here they lie alone and unsung, in the humblest of hilltop resting places."[19] To enter is to feel the past present, a stillness that is close to wonder. Like Wayland's Smithy it is sacred space but of a gentler kind. Churches carry meaning in their arches, spaces, light, and history.

It was the Victorians who most emphatically restored the idea of the beauty of holiness. Writing in 1837 the architect William Bardwell saw church buildings as "a witness to the truth of the invisible world."[20] For him "every Church tower that rises above the trees is a hieroglyphic of the word GOD."[21] Thomas Chamberlain, the Anglo-Catholic vicar of St. Thomas' Oxford, put the central assumption splendidly. God, he said, has always used the "beauty of color and form to ravish the eye" and thus change lives.[22] The Anglo-Catholic movement and architects like Pugin were central to this. But as William Whyte, in his illuminative study of the Victorian recovery of sacred space, observes "so widespread was this new view of architecture that it transcended Oxford and Cambridge, the Tractarians

---

19. Jenkins, *England's Thousand Best Churches*, 644.
20. Bardwell, *Temples, Ancient and Modern*, 14.
21. Bardwell, *Temples, Ancient and Modern*, 29. .
22. Chamberlain, *Chancel*, 18.

and the Ecclesiologists, the High Low and Broad Church Traditions."[23] The Nonconformist architect James Cubitt spoke for them all: "Every stone... tells in a universal language of the idea for which it was built."[24] Truth does not simply come through words. "No preacher... can be always preaching, no poem can be always reciting, no music can be always sounding in men's ears, but art is never silent."[25] Exactly as the highly rational Fosdick was to see later, Cubitt saw that, "there is a value in beauty as well as in truth; in feeling as well as in intellect."[26]

Not all were convinced. When Lion Walk Congregational Church in Colchester replaced its plain Round Meeting House of 1766 in 1863 by a neo-Gothic building in Caen stone it occasioned considerable controversy. Christians, declared a stoutly traditional member, J. A. Tabor, should feel ashamed to participate in the "vain-glorious erection for the worship of God of highly architectural and gorgeous edifices, with lofty and defiant towers."[27] He quoted a correspondent who wrote, "So they are building a spire to the new Lion Walk Chapel: Ah! These modern dissenters are spire mad! I like a good substantial neat building, but do not like this rage after the pomp of popery."[28] The obscurantist absurdity of that was apparent to most of the church. The last sermon in the old building by the Rev. T. W. Davids was titled, "Arise! Let us go hence."[29] Which they did. Tabor resigned his membership and may have felt vindicated when the top of the spire was first blown down by a storm in 1869 and then brought down by an earthquake in 1884.

Nonconformist Gothic is sometimes mocked. John Betjeman refers to:

> The Nonconformist spirelets
> And the Church of England spires.[30]

But there was often a freshness and variety about such churches, a freedom from Anglican stereotypes. And sometimes at least the Nonconformist spire could be deliberately built to be higher and more

---

23. Whyte, *Unlocking the Church*, 55.
24. Cubitt, *Church Design for Congregations*, 8.
25. Cubitt, *Nonconformist Church Building*, 3–4.
26. Cubitt, *Nonconformist Church Building*, 3–4.
27. Tabor, *Nonconformist Protest*, 4–5.
28. Blaxill, *History of Lion Walk*, 44.
29. Blaxill, *History of Lion Walk*, 44.
30. Betjeman, *Collected Poems*, 149.

prominent than the Church of England spirelet. The Lion Walk spire could be seen for miles around and was the most prominent of any Colchester Church. As far as one knows no one was corrupted by it, but the Colchester skyline had a reminder of the sacred.

Where they were right the Puritans were gloriously right, the church is not the building and God can be met with anywhere. But throughout history places have brought the spiritual into people's lives. Churches are not just boxes where you can sing and preach. They can have atmosphere. The beauty of a place can open our minds and hearts for an encounter with something beyond us, something holy or sacred. It can give us the sense that there's more going on in the world than just us. Mansfield and Riverside did that for me. King's College Chapel for John Betjeman. In a broadcast on the Home Service on Christmas Day 1947 he said, "I cannot believe I am surrounded by a purposeless universe." He tells of a carol service at King's. As the congregation waited for the service to begin, the first verse of "Once in Royal David's City" was sung by a boy treble beyond the screen. "It was clear, pure, distinct. And as I heard it, I knew once more—knew despite myself—that this story was the Truth."[31]

## THE CHURCH IN A DISENCHANTED WORLD

None of this is today as obvious as it once was. A great many churches have closed. The Methodists, for example, closed 310 churches between 2005 and 2010—a rate of more than one every week, and the expectation must be that many more will follow. The real problem, however, goes deeper. Buildings are texts which are read differently depending on the cultural context. Philip Larkin's post-Christian churchgoer entering a church building today will not see or feel or react to what they see in the way medieval people, or a Victorian would have done. We contextualize and experience what we see differently. Elizabeth Barrett Browning may be right that:

> Earth's crammed with heaven,
> And every common bush afire with God.

But she is definitely right when she adds, "But only he who sees takes off his shoes."[32]

---

31. Quoted in Meara, *Passion for Places*, 36–37.
32. Nicholson and Lee, *Oxford Book of English Mystical Verse*, 146.

## SACRED SPACE—A SYMPHONY IN STONE

It was Mansfield College again which brought this home most forcibly to me. After I retired, I was invited to preach at the commemoration service. It was not the happiest of occasions. It rained, the champagne reception was moved indoors, and I was only just well enough to be there and croaked my way through the sermon. But more than that—times had changed. The declining number of ordinands in the United Reformed Church meant this was no longer a theological college and a permanent private hall but a full college of the university. The principal was no longer a URC minister—its church past clearly behind it. The Gothic chapel, with its statues and stained glass, which had so moved me when a student, was now used as the college dining hall. In the side chapel, where morning prayers used to be, there were the urns from which food was ladled out. For the service, the chairs were temporarily side-lined, but the urns remained. Later we had dinner in the chapel. "It's just wonderful," the principal said to me, "now the students can all eat together." "Yes" said the senior tutor, "it's a great teaching opportunity; none of them have any idea who these people in the stained-glass windows were."

Inevitably churches are now seen in a secular context. Simon Jenkins is a newspaper columnist who was Chairman of the National Trust and wrote *England's Thousand Best Churches*. Though he seldom refers to it, his father Daniel Jenkins was a United Reformed Church minister, so he is a son of the manse. He writes, "To most people today a church is a puzzling place."[33] From his background he understands their religious significance, but he sees no future for it. "England's churches can survive—but the religion will have to go."[34] He suggests handing them over to parish councils and converting them to communal activities such as concert halls, post offices, village shops, farmers markets, cafes, or e-shopping collection points. It is all eminently practical and indeed something like this has happened to many closed, or only partially used churches. The former Stockwell Congregational Church in Colchester is now offices, and its Junior Church building is a children's play center, with a license for a night club in part of the building. A few hundred yards away, the Norman All Saints Church is a Natural History Museum, Holy Trinity Church with its fine Saxon tower is a café, St. Mary at the Walls is the Colchester Arts Centre and Headgate Congregational Church is now the Headgate Theatre. All these uses are in their own way admirable—a continued useful life for

33. Jenkins, *Thousand Best Churches*, ix.
34. *Guardian*, Oct 22, 2015.

the building after there were no longer viable congregations for them. For the religious believer none of these new uses constitute a no-go area for God, who may be disclosed in children's play or drama or the relation of one person with another. But sacred space they are not.

Even when churches remain as places of worship their architecture is secularized. When new churches are built often the economics determine they are multi-purpose utilitarian halls very similar to community centers. In Birkenhead I preached quite often at the imposing neo-Gothic Oxton Congregational Church, opened in 1858. By the time I preached there, however, the congregation had so shrunk that the tiny handful of worshipers met in the rather shabby vestry. In Halstead, when the imposing Victorian Church became too large for the United Reformed Church congregation, they moved into an old doctor's surgery. Frequently economic viability involves churches being built as part of a complex of shops or offices. Lion Walk Colchester offers a perfect example of this. The Victorian Gothic building was replaced in 1984 when a new shopping development took place, and the new church building was placed above the shops. Although the old tower was retained, separated from the new building, this meant it was quite easy to walk past the church without being aware it was there. River Island's clothing display draws the eye, not the church. On the positive side the simplicity of the new building might have allowed Tabor to come back into membership!

Changing styles of architecture reflected changing times. By the mid-twentieth century traditional formal church buildings seemed "old-fashioned." In an age in which the hymnwriter Richard Jones could ask a congregation to praise the "God of concrete, God of steel," minimalist architecture in which form followed function seemed more appropriate than Gothic arches. Some of these churches were inspiring but many were less successful. The much-praised concrete soon became associated not with modernity and progress but with ugliness and inhumanity. As Simon Jenkins says, "God was a poor modernist. How else to explain His inflicting the Church of the Good Shepherd with St John in West Bromwich? . . . The church is a brick blockhouse without form or charm. The best to be said is that it would have been even worse had it waited for the 70s. At least brick is better than pre-stressed concrete."[35] There were exceptions. Jenkins mentions Robinson College Cambridge with its fine stained glass by John Piper and Patrick Reyntiens and a neighborhood church like Castle Hill

---

35. *Guardian*, April 5, 2006.

URC Ipswich, its high roof reminiscent of the traditional roofs of Suffolk churches and its attractive use of colored glass, shows concrete is not incompatible with beauty or a sense of worship. Marc Chagall's windows at All Saints Tuedley fill the church with rich color and Ceri Richard's painting in the Sacrament Chapel at Liverpool Metropolitan Cathedral shows how, in the right context, abstract art offers profundity. But we should not overstress the exceptions. Too often churches from this period were grim grey concrete facades, already fortunately needing to be replaced.

The Roman Catholic Michael Rose gave the title *Ugly as Sin* to his book on modern church architecture.[36] That is far too sweeping but his subtitle, *Why They Changed Our Churches from Sacred Spaces to Meeting Places*, touches a raw nerve. At the other theological end of the spectrum the great American megachurches reveal the unmistakable influence of modern commercial designs of office parks and shopping malls. Often, they look like an office building with the worship space like a lecture hall with video screens. Charles Trueheart describes it:

> No spires. No crosses. No robes. No clerical collars. No hard pews. No kneelers. No biblical gobbledygook. . . . No pipe organs. No dreary 18th-century hymns. No forced solemnity . . . Centuries of Christian habit are deliberately being abandoned clearing the way for new contemporary forms of worship and belonging.[37]

In Southampton, Above Bar Church is just that kind of building, with a tiered sanctuary centering on a lectern exactly like a lecture theatre. Whereas older churches had been prominent, newer ones often merged unobtrusively with their surroundings. In Sutton, where the neo-Gothic Trinity Church was the other side of the road from the architecturally much praised Sutton Baptist Church, opened in 1934, I more than once had to tell people asking where the Baptist Church was, that they were standing in front of it.

All this was given theological justification. If the church was the people did the building really matter? As Sandi Villarreal says in the social justice magazine, *Sojourners*,

> I believe there is a call to return to the roots of Christianity. Especially in this time of economic instability, what need have we for fancy buildings and expensive programming? The word of

---

36. Rose, *Ugly as Sin*.
37. Trueheart, "Welcome to the Next Church," 37.

God is just as true in my living room or in a coffee shop as it is in a 1,000-seat sanctuary.[38]

The mood is that of a United Reformed Church recently which wished to alter its building, arguing that it is under-used, in that it is only used once a week. It is the old Puritan protest again in a new form. Just as then, it's right in what it affirms but misses something central. Of course, you can pray in a lost property office, but the claim that the building doesn't matter is intellectually frivolous. As Gladstone once put it, "If it has been ordained that the senses should be channels of a large part of our perceptions, why should we not make them monitors of heavenly truth, instead of leaving them avenues to be occupied by things mischievous, things secular, or things indifferent."[39] Light, color, music, and other forms of beauty all mediate the holy. I do not for a moment suggest that the wonder of God cannot be experienced in box-like utilitarian churches. It can be and is. But it is rather like playing the piano with one hand. No doubt it can be done, but why would you out of choice?

## REIMAGINING THE TRANSCENDENT

This is not an easy time for churches; indeed it is a pretty grim time and getting grimmer. But seeking to secularize church into a social service agency or removing Jesus from the context of belief in God and affirming him as a secular social justice advocate is no answer. There is no simple way of changing the culture but the transcendent remains at the heart of religious faith, the power of it can reach us when we listen to music or walk in the hills or feel the touch of the hand of the one we love, or are filled with the rapture of a spring morning. As William James concluded in his *Varieties of Religious Experience*, "No account of the universe in its totality can be final which leaves these forms of consciousness quite disregarded . . . at any rate, they forbid a premature closing of our accounts with reality."[40] The church's task is not to limit its horizon to an exclusively secular view of life but to recover the confidence to speak coherently and honestly of the transcendent.

One thing we need to do is clarify what we mean by transcendence. No one is more helpful here than the German/American theologian Paul

---

38. *Sojourners*, Mar 9, 2012.
39. Gladstone, *Church Principles*, 337.
40. James, *Varieties of Religious Experience*, 388.

Tillich (1886–1965). Serving with the German Army in the First World War he recognized the deep gulf between the soldier's world and the faith they had grown up with.[41] Now he plunged into the abyss, and his mental world was shattered. His old view of God had been of a God who controls human life, determining fortunes, like a superior version of us, all-powerful and all-knowing. Such simplistic faith crumbled when faced with the realities of life. In the trenches such a God was simply not there, any more than such a God can be found in science or history. But that was not the end but the real beginning of his faith journey. In 1918, when in the Kaiser Friedrich Museum in Berlin, he saw Botticelli's painting "Madonna with Singing Angels":

> As I stood there, bathed in the beauty . . . Something of the divine source of all things came through to me. I turned away shaken. That moment has affected my whole life, given me the key for interpretation of human existence, brought vital joy and spiritual truth.[42]

Transcendence was not contact with a supernatural being. "The protest of atheism, against such a highest person, is correct."[43] For Tillich transcendence is not contact with another world, but "an encounter with the holy, an encounter which has an ecstatic character."[44] As John Robinson says, "This, I believe, is Tillich's great contribution to theology—the reinterpretation of transcendence in a way which preserves its reality while detaching it from the projection of supernaturalism."[45] For Tillich it was Botticelli, for others it might be the experience of love, or the sense of moral obligation, or beauty in other forms, or the life of Christ, or the experience of worship or prayer, or simply reflection on what makes our life what it is. All these can be transcendent moments which take us beyond ourselves, not to another world but to the heart of this one. They open the possibility that, as W. H. Auden puts it,

> Space is the Whom our loves are needed by,
> Ours is the choice of How to love and Why.[46]

---

41. For a fuller discussion of Tillich's experiences in the First World War see Camroux, *Keeping Alive the Rumour of God*, ch. 3.
42. Manning, *Cambridge Companion to Paul Tillich*, 155–56.
43. Tillich, *Systematic Theology*, vol. 1, 245.
44. Tillich, *Systematic Theology*, vol. 2, 8.
45. Robinson, *Honest to God*, 56.
46. Robinson, *Difference*, 29.

This is the absolute heart of Christian belief, and it cannot be let go. However difficult it is to speak of, we must try.

Peripheral to the culture though it is, unacknowledged by most secular discourse, the transcendent is still part of human experience. It is difficult to be certain how widespread religious experience is. One survey, reported on by David Hay in 2000, found no less than 38 percent of people who had experienced an awareness of the presence of God, and a total of 76 percent who had some kind of religious and spiritual experience.[47] However a wide variety of kinds of experience fall under the general rubric of religious experience. The concept is vague, and the multiplicity of kinds of experiences makes it difficult to draw general conclusions. Such experiences may be significant for individuals but the fact that they mostly do not lead on to any activity or collective worship suggests they are peripheral to life. Nonetheless there is no doubt that such experiences do still occur and can be meaningful and even life-changing. And some places too can still have a special quality to them. The theologian Marcus Borg lost his childhood faith but later rediscovered faith anew when he felt the wonder of God in the mountains of the Pacific Northwest:

> In my mid-thirties I had a number of experiences of what I now recognise as "nature mysticism" . . . marked by what the Jewish theologian Abraham Herschel called "radical amazement," moments of transformed perception in which the earth is "filled with the glory of God," shining with a radiant presence.[48]

There is nothing unusual about such experiences. I was talking to a man at a wedding reception recently. "I'm not really a religious man," he said. "But the other day I was up Ben More on the Isle of Mull. And there was no sound except the wind. And for the first time in my life, I thought I knew why people believe in God." After another such moment, also in the Hebrides, a poet wrote: "In such a place as this the very wind is like a prayer." For me, Tennyson Down on the Isle of Wight, Pulpit Hill at Oban, and the great skies of Norfolk have all had this quality. Such moments do not prove the existence of God. As Auden says,

---

47. Robinson, *Difference*, 11.
48. Borg, *Meeting Jesus*, 14.

## SACRED SPACE—A SYMPHONY IN STONE

> All proofs or disproofs that we tender
> Of His existence are returned
> Unopened to the sender.[49]

But something of life is opened up, which materialism alone is inadequate to answer.

And churches too can still be sacred space. Before writing *England's Thousand Best Churches*, Simon Jenkins says that he had no sense of the quality of holiness that religious believers suggest churches can express. By the time he had finished he was not quite so sure. Late one summer he found himself at the Church of Up Marden in the Sussex Downs where villagers had worshiped for a thousand years. Now their faith communicated itself to him:

> I could not be immune to the spirits of such a place. I do not experience these spirits in theatres or assembly halls . . . Yet I find them in a wild hillside chapel or in the echoing aisle of a Gothic minster . . . They do not force me to my knees, but they whisper to me softly, as they did to Philip Larkin, bidding him 'to take off my cycle-clips in awkward reverence.'[50]

Churches can still speak. David Brooks, a *New York Times* columnist who describes himself as neither believing in God nor an atheist, tells of walking into Grace Episcopal Church on a busy street corner in lower Manhattan. "To leave the sidewalk and enter the church is to walk into a deeper story. The Kingdom of Heaven is announced on the facade. You sink into a hushed reverence inside the door as the world falls away." It is time to rediscover churches not as heritage sites or prospective post offices but as sacred space, places of wonder where a skeptical society can rediscover the transcendent. Churches represent an alternative set of transforming values and offer an experience of beauty which, like music and poetry, is still capable of taking us out of ourselves. Of course, there is always the danger that the building itself will become what we care about, as John Betjeman saw:

> Illuminated missals—spires—
> Wide screens and decorated quires—
> All these I loved, and on my knees
> I thanked myself for knowing these.[51]

---

49. Auden, *Selected Poems*, 238.
50. Jenkins, *Best Churches*, xxix.
51. Betjeman, *Collected Poems*, 131.

But it certainly can be otherwise.

My last pastorate was Trinity United Reformed and Methodist Church in Sutton, which opened in 1907 as Trinity Wesleyan Church. One of its ministers, the second finest Methodist hymnwriter Fred Pratt Green, in what may be his worst poem, wrote:

> They built a church in a first class suburb;
> Its proportions were noble, its site superb,
> They built it in several Gothic styles.
> Its tower and corona could be seen for miles.[52]

More soberly the Pikes District Directory for 1908 says, "The building, which is of Kentish rag and Bath stone, is designed after the style of the fifteenth century Gothic, the outstanding feature being the massive tower with a slender spire supported by flying buttresses."[53] Both are right about the 140-foot crown and lantern tower, an unusual design found in only nine churches in Britain, most notably St. Giles Cathedral Edinburgh, Coats Memorial Baptist Church in Glasgow, Newcastle Cathedral, and Wren's Church of St. Dunstan's in the East. The most prominent church in Sutton, Trinity, towers over the Anglican spirelets. Architecturally there is little original about it. In his *Chapels of England*, Christopher Wakeling calls it "noble, if unadventurous,"[54] whereas Sutton Baptist Church across the road, is "exciting" and "exceptional in its radical paraphrase of Gothic forms."[55] But as a place of worship Trinity excels.

Everyone driving through Sutton can see it, people looking for a church naturally gravitate to it, and the building induces awe and wonder. When I was conducting wedding rehearsals people would enter it for the first time, the church quiet, empty, and sometimes partially lit. Very frequently they would be moved by the beauty of it, "What a church," they would say to me. It was ideal for organ recitals, concerts, and significant acts of worship. For me the most powerful service of the year (rather against my theology) was the Candlelit Christmas Midnight service for which it was always packed. Towards the end all lights were extinguished, and I would read the Prologue to John's Gospel with only the one Christ candle burning. "The light shines in the darkness, and the darkness did not overcome it" (John 1:5). Then

---

52. Howard, *History of Trinity Church*, 13.
53. Howard, *History of Trinity Church*, 24
54. Wakeling, *Chapels of England*, 185.
55. Wakeling, *Chapels of England*, 226–7.

young people would light their candles from the Christ candle and share the light with the congregation until the church was lit with three hundred candles, and we sang, "O come, all ye faithful." Year after year it was a truly awesome moment.

> Yea, Lord, we greet thee,
> born this happy morning;
> Jesus, to Thee be glory given.[56]

I was occasionally asked by fellow ministers whether it was not a distraction from the church's mission to have such a building. I tried to tell them, usually with little success, that the prominence of the building was a powerful support for evangelism, and its beauty helped incarnate the wonder of God. Speaking at the Centenary Dinner Clyde Binfield saw the point. It is, he said,

> a building that for any rational, present-day church purposes is probably as inappropriate as could be and yet which is such a symbol, such a landmark, such an opportunity because of its grand unsuitability, as we should die for.[57]

One of the more recent and interesting developments is that despite it being a Nonconformist church where such things are not the tradition, increasing numbers of people want to come into the building to say a prayer and light a candle.

If churches were ever to fall completely out of use, no doubt people would still experience the sacred elsewhere. But the loss to Christian faith would be incalculable. And so would the loss to society in general. All across Britain, or for that matter Europe and America, are thousands of special buildings, many but not all beautiful, which offer spiritual meaning. Gothic and neo-Gothic churches and cathedrals, the white wooden churches of New England, the Baroque churches of the Counter-Reformation, the Byzantine churches of the Orthodox, the country chapels, and the great town churches. Once they dominated the landscape as Christian faith. Today, even when they are still open, they are often overlooked by tower blocks, offices, or shopping centers which reflect the commercial logic of consumer capitalism. As Angela Tilby only slightly unfairly puts it, "I sometimes think that our public buildings, and our soulless flats and

---

56. United Reformed Church, *Rejoice and Sing*, No. 160.
57. Binfield, *Trinity Church, Sutton*, 3.

offices, are witness only to the godlessness of our age, telling us that we are essentially machines to be packaged into rectangular spaces."[58]

Churches remind us of less tangible values, dimensions of reality that are not quantifiable: the numinous, the holy, wonder, mystery, awe. Roger Kennedy, former director of the National Museum of American History at the Smithsonian, in his *American Churches*, wrote, "Any visitor to New York who stands on Fifth Avenue between Rockefeller Centre and 57th Street can see that, in the glassy shadow of the skyscrapers, there lurks an older way of stating reality."[59] The reference is to St. Patrick's Catholic Cathedral, St. Thomas Episcopal Church, and Fifth Avenue Presbyterian Church. These all are about something quite different, the struggle to express the inexpressible—to create what Le Corbusier called, in reference to his great chapel at Ronchamp, France, "ineffable space."[60] In the midst of a consumerist society, they offer a place for the human spirit, the sense there is more to life that can be felt by believer and unbeliever alike.

You can experience something of this in most places blessed with churches. In Chicago, Fourth Presbyterian Church was opened in 1914 with its sanctuary designed by the foremost Gothic architect in America, Ralph Adams Cram. The September 1914 issue of *The Architectural Record* devoted a major review to Cram's new church and called Fourth Presbyterian Church "a living, breathing, spiritual thing . . . a marvel of grace, beauty, and dignity." It is located in what is called the Magnificent Mile, directly across Michigan Avenue from the John Hancock Center—surrounded by skyscrapers and hotels and retail department stores such as Bloomingdale's where you can buy a Salvatore Ferragamo Leather Satchel for £2200 ($2800). But Fourth Presbyterian witnesses to something else. As its former minister John Buchanan says, "We do provide a balance, an alternate reality statement about transcendence and holiness and mystery and meaning . . . when I walk from the busy, noisy sidewalk into the silent stillness of church, I have always experienced and experience still something of the Holy."[61] Churches are not just wonderful architecture but an entrée to a deeper wonder, a fuller view of our humanity. As George Herbert says,

---

58. *Church Times*, Sep 18, 2020.
59. Kennedy, *American Churches*.
60. Le Corbusier, *New World of Space*, 8.
61. Buchanan, "Truly Precious."

Yet in thy temple thou dost him afford
This glorious and transcendent place,
To be a window, through thy grace.[62]

---

62. Herbert, *English Poems*, 84.

# 4

# JESUS—NO STORY SO DIVINE

CHURCHES ARE WIDELY DIVERSE in worship, life, and belief, but one thing they have in common is that they are places where the story of Jesus is told. His face gazes down from innumerable stained-glass windows or domes, he is at the center of the liturgy and the preaching. Christians justify this by making the most astonishing claim about him: that to see him is to see God. In the poetic words of Sydney Carter, in him:

> The king of all creation,
> Had a cradle on the earth.[1]

As ever there are ambiguities here. Our accounts of the past are kept alive through memory and interpretation and have an inevitable fluidity and mutability. As we change, so do they. The past is never fully recoverable. In this case there are relatively few certainties about Jesus and who he was. There were radically different takes on him from the beginning and there still are. Often, as we look at the probabilities, there will be an open-minded hesitancy rather than a clear-cut certainty. This is not particular to Jesus; it is the nature of history. But it is from this imperfectly known life that there comes a living stream of history, teaching, myth, music, poetry, and art, which gives us a story which can transform the way we see ourselves and in whom Christians see God. He has provided us with the greatest story in Western civilization.

The chances of all this coming out of the life of an obscure Galilean carpenter who was executed ignominiously by a colonial power, and barely

---

1. United Reformed Church, *New Church Praise*, 20.

mentioned by any contemporary source, are so slight as to be virtually non-existent. That we do remember him is because of the church. It was his small community of disciples whose conviction that death had not ended their relationship with him who reignited his movement when it seemed extinct. It was in this community that his life and words were passed on and later became the basis of the Gospels, which are the only accounts we have of his life. It was the church which explored the significance of his life and formulated doctrines like the Trinity, which became the lens through which his life was viewed. When the Bible was finally put together, a process that was not complete until the late fourth century, it was the church which finally determined which books were included and which were not. It was in the church that, through the centuries, his story was called to mind as it became the subject of liturgy, preaching and music, and art. I quite frequently hear people say, "I love Jesus, but I can't stand the church." I sympathize with this and often feel like it myself. But those who say it ought in honesty to reflect that without the church it is most unlikely that we would know anything about Jesus at all. He is the church's gift to the world. Whether we like it or not Jesus and the church cannot be separated. No church, no Jesus.

## THE GOOD MAN JESUS

There are two parts to Jesus' significance. Firstly, this is the life of an amazingly good man and astounding teacher. In the Acts of the Apostles the memory of Jesus is that "he went about doing good" (Acts 10:38). That must be the overwhelming impression we still have of him. Even Richard Dawkins once wrote an article entitled "Atheists for Jesus."[2] Jesus' warm compassion is not in doubt and the stories that seem most typical of him see him at his most remarkable. In the Gospel stories he takes the initiative: he intercedes for the woman about to be stoned for adultery, he invites the tax collector to come down out of a tree and go to lunch, he welcomes those nobody wants—prostitutes, sinners, the unclean—invites them to table and sits down and eats with them. He makes a member of another race and faith our exemplar in his most well-loved parable and tells of a father who goes down the road to welcome a lost child home. His openness to others, his radical forgiveness, his willingness to challenge the powerful, and his dependence on God, remain a challenging inspiration. The actor Alec

---

2. Dawkins, "Atheists for Jesus."

McCowen once did a one-man show which simply consisted of reading the Gospel of Mark. The experience led him to say, "Whether or not you are a 'believer,' it is impossible to study St. Mark carefully and not know—without a shadow of doubt—that something amazing happened in Galilee two thousand years ago."[3] To put it very simply, for 2000 years all sorts and conditions of people have lived better lives because of his influence on them. I know this because, deeply imperfect as my own life has been, I am one of them.

It is difficult to be precise about how exactly Jesus came to touch my life because his story was part of the milieu in which I grew up. I was born in a family steeped in Congregationalism, and at Shrub End Congregational Church in Colchester I was presented with a view of Jesus by the minister, the Rev. Frank Mead, which I now know was heavily influenced by the great preachers of the day, Leslie Weatherhead and Harry Emerson Fosdick, whose sermons often came to me in redacted form. Introducing a book of his sermons Weatherhead wrote, "If, my dear reader, any sentence in this volume brings you near enough to Christ so that you see Him and hear the whisper of his voice, it will not matter if the preacher is forgotten."[4] Something like that happened to me, I did hear the whisper of his voice. It made Christ real to me, and made me love him, and gave me the sense that, if God was like Jesus, God was my friend. This evangelical liberalism remains the core of my faith.

Later I explored my faith more academically, doing both O- and A-level Bible Knowledge, which was a great deal more interesting than it sounds. Through the influence of theologians like Rudolf Bultmann I learned to apply critical thinking to the New Testament stories, understanding how the traditions had been collected and influenced by the needs of the church. This seemed to make it possible to make at least some attempt to grasp what was early, and what was late, in the tradition. Through Bultmann too came my understanding of Jesus as the proclaimer of the kingdom, and I was fascinated by the debate between the Bultmann tradition and Mansfield scholars like George Caird and C. H. Dodd as to how literally we should take Jesus' eschatological hope. All of this helped to ground the Jesus story in history and reality and a context of honest questioning, but in no sense did it make Jesus less inspiring, rather the reverse. I came to see there was no question you couldn't ask, there was no truth on which you had to

3. *Sunday Times Weekly Review*, Feb 17, 1980.
4. Weatherhead, *Eternal Voice*, 11.

compromise. As John Robinson, the author of *Honest to God* and my first real theological hero, put it:

> A Christian ... has nothing to fear in the truth.... it is a living and growing reality. And therefore he is free to follow the truth *wherever* it leads.[5]

At school too, outside the classroom, I read *Honest to God*'s powerful presentation of Jesus as "The Man for Others"—"It is in Jesus, and Jesus alone, that there is nothing of self to be seen, but solely the ultimate, unconditional, love of God."[6] I came to see Jesus as someone of huge sensitivity to the needs of others, who jumped out of his time into mine. This commitment and understanding were deepened by the worship I was taking part in Sunday by Sunday, by Sydney Carter's "Lord of the Dance" and moving traditional hymns like Isaac Watts "When I Survey the Wondrous Cross" or Samuel Crossman's "My Song is Love Unknown":

> Here might I stay and sing,
> No story so divine.
> Never was love, dear King,
> Never was grief like Thine.[7]

All of this became part of my essential criteria for determining right and wrong and offered a radical social agenda. Peace and justice were achievable. Ending world poverty was the great task before us. Ecumenism and women's rights were inherently gospel values. I could throw my hat in the air for racial justice, singing "We Shall Overcome" on all possible occasions. Marching down the Mall in Washington, D.C., Peter, Paul and Mary led the singing: "Black and white together."

Today how do I feel about this youthful commitment? Unquestionably it was all more complex than I understood. Trying to determine what is original Jesus and what are church interpretations of his life is frequently impossible. How much, for example, of his greatest parables is original to Jesus and how much a tribute to the literary skills of Luke? The Sermon on the Mount is a compilation put together by Matthew, not Jesus. It is Matthew who chooses what to include and shapes the teaching. In all honesty, is there a single saying of Jesus which we can be absolutely certain, beyond any possibility of doubt, that we have it in its original form? At

---

5. Robinson, *Can We Trust the New Testament?*, 133.
6. Robinson, *Honest to God*, 74.
7. United Reformed Church, *Rejoice and Sing*, 207.

many points of his life the facts are difficult to determine, the line between teaching and interpretation, history, and myth unclear. Did he think he was Son of God? I am not certain. When he called himself Son of Man, what did he mean? Scholars differ!

None of this disturbs me greatly. That there is a unique human being at the heart of the Jesus story no serious historian doubts. Through New Testament scholarship we can attempt to trace the development of the tradition prior to the composition of the gospels. It is clear we are dealing with a man who came to be viewed as God, not a myth projected back into history. I can take the uncertainty which goes with history, confident at the core of all this is a real person, whose life still has the power to inspire. I can listen to his story without caring too much whether the words are his or a reflection on him. In the Gospels we find a unique human being, himself, and no one else, set in an entirely credible historical context.

Today we tend to look back at the past with huge condescension, secure in our sense of our own superiority and relative moral virtue. Churchill held imperialist views, Nelson had links with the West Indies and therefore with the slave trade, the early pioneers of the social gospel were not always alert to racism or gay rights. Often all we are really saying is that all periods of history have their moral blind spots just as we have ours. These critiques are often more than a little self-righteous. But what is interesting to me is how difficult it is to pin such a critique on Jesus.

Not infrequently in my early days of ministry I would challenge congregations to show me anywhere, where after 2000 years, Jesus' moral vision could be challenged? No one ever did, but I now think they could have done so. As is inevitable Jesus certainly used some phrases and concepts which have not always lasted well. There are traces of something akin to racial superiority in Jesus' reference to the gentiles as "dogs" (Mark 7:27), though the story ends with his breaking through his prejudice. I am uneasy about some of the language he uses about hell (e.g., Matt 23:33), though Gehenna is certainly not the hell imagined by sadistic medieval theologians, and it is open to argument exactly how much of this language is metaphorical rather than literal. Nonetheless I would not personally use it today. But what really strikes me is how few such examples there are, and how amazingly morally powerful the teaching of Jesus still is. There is barely a recorded encounter of Jesus in the Gospels where he is not crossing some form of social or religious barrier in order to empower people and confront prejudice. He is open to women and to the socially and racially excluded. The Sermon on the Mount is not outdated.

For fifteen years Harvey Cox taught a course at Harvard University called Jesus and the Moral Life. It was one of the most popular in the University often enrolling over 1000 students a semester, including Jewish and non-religious students as well as Christians of various kinds. Often, they would argue with him and among themselves. But then he would come to the climax of the sermon, the section on forgiveness which begins, "You have heard that it was said, 'You shall love your neighbor and hate your enemy.' But I say to you, 'Love your enemies and pray for those who persecute you, so that you may be children of your Father in heaven'" (Matt 5:43–45). Over the years Cox says he found the students did not want to argue about this.

> So eventually, when I reached these verses in class, I simply paused after I read them. Invariably there was a profound silence in the room. Why offer a commentary on the Mona Lisa? If the Sermon on the Mount was Jesus' Fifth Symphony this was his central theme. Why say more? Commenting on it, or even discussing it, seemed almost superfluous. It still does.[8]

What makes this even more powerful is Jesus not only talks of forgiveness but lives it.

At the heart of the message of Jesus are the parables, which make up 35 percent of his teaching in the synoptic Gospels. Many of these stories, such as the good samaritan, the prodigal son, the sheep and the goats, Dives and Lazarus, or the grains of wheat which fall on different kinds of soil are some of the great stories of our literature. They are not always simple to understand. What are we to make of the dishonest steward, which Cox calls the "The Tale of the Crooked CEO"?[9] His students were bewildered by this, and preachers are not fond of it. Sometimes the stories may leave us perplexed, as no doubt was originally the case. Often it may well have been Jesus' intention to leave questions in people's minds rather than conclusions. It is very noticeable that when the evangelists have tagged on explanations to the stories, they are almost always less interesting than the stories themselves. But the stories are vivid, deeply morally powerful, and challenging. As a student in the 1960s it was the parable of the sheep and the goats which had the most influence on me—what counted was not what

8. Cox, *Jesus*, 137.
9. Cox, *Jesus*, 162.

you said you believed, but how you responded to human need. As someone who quite often can't remember where sayings come in the gospels, the words in Matthew 25 bring it instantly to mind: "Truly I tell you, just as you did it to one of the least of these who are members of my family, you did it to me" (Matt 25:40). Jim Wallis, who has been a prophetic voice in evangelical Christianity, says this parable was fundamental in his life:

> Matthew 25:31–46 is my own conversion text, the scripture that brought me to Christ a long time ago out of the radical student movement. It's also been a converting text for many others here at Sojourners over the years.[10]

The story of the good samaritan, so beloved of Sunday schools over the years, has a similar strikingly radical message: that caring is more important than nationality or religious origin. The message is "Don't ask who your neighbor is, simply be one to the person in need." In the social idealism of the 1960s this was spelled out in the songs of Sydney Carter:

> When I needed a neighbour, were you there,
> were you there?
> When I needed a neighbour, were you there?
>
> And the creed and the colour
> and the name won't matter,
> Were you there?[11]

When it comes to the central question of what God is like, the parable of the prodigal son has been hugely influential. Donatello sculpted it. Chaucer loved it. Rembrandt painted it twice. It was Dickens's favorite tale. Thoreau claimed that it was the greatest piece of literature ever written. Lives have been changed by it. For centuries this parable has been called *evangelium in evagelio*—the gospel within the gospel. One scholar wrote, "While Jesus was not a philosopher or theologian in the accepted sense, his parables alone provide material that neither the philosopher nor the theologian can exhaust. This is the mark of supreme genius."[12] There is more

---

10. *Sojourners*, Nov 2015. *Sojourners* is a magazine linked to the Sojourners Community, a Christian social justice organization which began at Trinity Evangelical Divinity School in Deerfield, Illinois, in the early 1970s when a handful of students began meeting to discuss the relationship between their faith and political issues, particularly the Vietnam War.

11. Methodist Church, *Singing the Faith*, 256.

12. Smith, *Jesus of the Parables*, 19.

complexity in this story than you might imagine, but the central image is powerful and unambiguous. The father rushes down the road to welcome his son home—this is how God is for us. Unlike the vengeful, vicious gods of much human imagination, God is found in love and forgiveness. Jesus challenges materialism, nationalism, and exclusive religion in the name of a compassionate God:

> Listen as he says that whoever receives a little child receives him and the God who is in him.
> Listen as he says love your enemy.
> Listen as he says love your neighbor.
> Listen as he tells a story about a neighbor, wounded, lying by the road, and the Good Samaritan who stops and helps.
> Listen as he says forgive those who hurt you, turn the other cheek to those who strike you.
> Listen as he says if you give your life away for my sake, you will find it.
> Listen as from the Cross he says, "Father, forgive them, for they know not what they do" (Luke 23.34).[13]

It is very hard to fault the moral passion of his life.

Jesus' impact on our culture and history has been profound, helping shape our most basic sense of right and wrong. As Paul Vallely[14] shows, when his teaching entered the Roman world, it transformed the way the poor were seen and the responsibilities society had to them. Christians picked up the abandoned babies who were simply left in the gutters to die and the church became an orphanage for the unwanted babies. Christians were conspicuous because they cared for those who were expendable: widows, orphans, the aged and infirm. The medieval system of church-organized almsgiving came from Christian belief, as did the idea of public education provided by the community for all children which emerged out of the Reformation, in Geneva led by John Calvin and in Scotland by John Knox. Jesus' influence continues to inspire both social concern and individual morality, including in recent times opposition to racism and apartheid, the search for individual human rights and peace, and practical help for the poor through organizations such as Christian Aid. Nelson Mandela went to two Methodist missionary schools. In what we might call an intended compliment, Friedrich Nietzsche complained that Christianity,

---

13. Revised form of original from John Buchanan sermon, "What About Jesus?" Presbyterian Church Chicago, February 22, 2009.

14. Vallely, *Philanthropy*, 28

had given Europe ideals of compassion and equality and "such phantoms as the dignity of man, the dignity of labour."[15]

It is not simple to apply the ethics of Jesus to our own time. There is a wide chasm between his world and ours, nicely summarized by Harvey Cox: "He was then, we are now."[16] Many of our concerns were not his, and some of his are not ours. The eschatological framework of his teaching can be very difficult for us to understand. Simplistic attempts to solve our ethical dilemmas by asking "What would Jesus do?" (WWJD) are often unhelpful and sometimes dangerous. Frequently there will be differing opinions as what he would have done, and sometimes there is no obvious link between his dilemmas and ours. It is not merely that if you are interested in the ethics of in-vitro fertilization, it is not much use looking to Jesus for an answer. Even on such a fundamental question as to whether armed force can ever be justified, different people will honestly interpret Jesus differently. The truth is we will have to take a leap of imagination and understanding to make a connection between Jesus' time and our very different world, and we shall often not know if we have got this right. Jesus is not a handy store or resource-room for solutions to our problems. But his moral relevance remains as a source of inspiration and as way of reviewing, reconsidering, and revising our problems as well as our solutions, our questions, and our answers.

George Price developed the Price Equation. which claimed a mathematical proof of a link between character and genetic links within kinship groups. If so, it would have meant, he decided, that altruism is not a moral choice but a selfish and genetic mechanism to ensure the survival of one's gene pool. Price was horrified by his conclusion, and from being strongly anti-religious went through a conversion experience, telling friends he had "sort" of "encountered" Jesus, who had told him, "Give to everyone who asks you."[17] He started doing exactly that, practicing random acts of kindness, and inviting the homeless to share his house with him. In his life he sought to disprove his own theory. Through the centuries many have, in one way or another, "encountered Jesus" in a way which affected their lives and others. In my lifetime this includes Desmond Tutu, Martin Luther King, Dietrich Bonhoeffer, Reinhold Niebuhr, Peter Benenson (the Amnesty International founder), and Pope John XXIII, who were all

---

15. Holland, *Dominion*, 448.
16. Cox, *Jesus*, 14.
17. Vallely, *Philanthropy*, 3–4.

shaped by the moral teaching of Jesus. It really is the case that something amazing happened in Galilee two thousand years ago.

## JESUS—THE HUMAN FACE OF GOD

But being a great moral teacher is not Jesus' greatest significance. It is fine to find God in as many places as possible and not to limit our ideas to any one tradition. But if ideas of the numinous are not to be vacuous they need a unifying focus. And for the Christian that is what Jesus provides. Thomas H. Troeger was a hymn writer, preacher, homiletics professor, theologian, poet, musician, and author. In his childhood he received a daily double theological blessing: His mother would read from the Bible to him, and he'd listen with his father to Bach, Handel, or Haydn. He says that double exposure made him who he was.

> "Yes, my mother read the Bible to me every morning," he recalls. "'You need Jesus!' she would say. She was a strong churchgoer, a probing woman. And with my father every night I'd sit and listen to a Bach cantata or Haydn symphony, and those would be holy moments too. So I think these account for a deep belief in Jesus, but also an openness to the numinous in different ways."[18]

What has happened is that the life of Jesus has become the focus of a story of death and resurrection, through which people have come to understand not only their own lives but also the fundamental truth of God. John Robinson takes up a phrase of William Blake's, "the human form divine," to call Jesus "the human face of God."[19] It's in this context that the Bible presents him, that preachers talk of him, and that he is portrayed most frequently in great art or music. The life of a historical person becomes a redemption story in which God enters human history in a Galilean carpenter.

> That glorious Form ...
> He laid aside, and here with us to be,
> Forsook the courts of everlasting day,
> And chose with us a darksome house of mortal clay.[20]

---

18. Waddle, "Thomas H. Troeger."
19. Robinson, *Human Face of God*, 244.
20. Milton, *Poetical Works*, 65.

Rejected by the religious and political authorities he reveals the depth of his love, and of God's identification with us, by accepting death and then by rising again, he shatters death revealing that good is stronger than evil, love stronger than death. By offering us the story of God incarnate in a rejected nobody, all human values are turned upside down. "Many who are first will be last, and the last will be first" (Matt 19.30).

Generations have lived within this story, as Thomas Troeger did, understanding through it their place in the love of God and hope for the world. What if God is not who we thought? What if God is like Jesus? What if God is not about vengeance or power or ridiculous church systems of authority but is as we see God in Jesus—sacrificial love? What if the world's supposedly powerful are actually empty facades because the arc of history bends towards justice? That changes everything. This understanding of Jesus goes beyond anything he himself would have known or believed, but it is a story rooted in his life and in historical fact. It's a story parents can teach to children, a story preachers use to capture the imagination and artists give their lives to. It's a universal story of salvation.

Stories matter. The Jewish philosopher Edith Wyschogrod argues that despite their importance neither moral philosophies nor ethical principles motivate anyone; we are motivated by narratives. This exaggerates. The Sermon on the Mount has motivated lives as has reading Kant or Marx. But when truth is expressed in human life it most powerfully catches the imagination. Joan Didion gets to the heart of it:

> We tell ourselves stories in order to live... We live entirely... by the imposition of a narrative line upon disparate images. By the ideas with which we have learned to freeze the shifting phantasmagoria which is our actual experience.[21]

Stories allow us to find shape and significance in the confusing mix of life. From Genesis onwards the Bible is full of stories that offer us meaning. Some of these stories may be fiction, some may be myth, some may be fact, often we may not be entirely sure what they are, but they tell us who we are.

A first example of this is the birth stories in Matthew and Luke. A pure virgin is addressed by an angel, a supernatural star leads wise men from afar, an angelic choir heralds the birth of God's son to shepherds out in the fields. If you are being mundane of course this is not exactly how it was—it is life dramatized and mythologized to reveal a world saturated with the

---

21. Didion, *White Album*, 1.

divine. "This is the irrational season," says Madeleine L'Engle, "when love blooms bright and wild."[22] The nativity stories are like an overture to an opera. You get a preview of the themes you are going to meet, a taste of what's to come which sets the mood. That there is no room in the inn anticipates the rejection Jesus will ultimately meet, the Magi from the east the way the gospel will go into the whole world, the shepherds the promise that the gospel is for the poor, the outcasts, and the marginalized, the flight into Egypt a first pointer that this is the new Moses. And then there is the Virgin Birth. It is most unlikely this is a historical fact. Stories of supernatural births were part of the cultural idioms of the ancient world by which they introduced great lives. Buddha, Zoroaster, Ra, Pythagoras, Plato, Romulus and Remus, and Augustus Caesar also had special births. In the case of Jesus, the Gospels refer to Joseph as his father, and the story is not in the earliest sources. It does not seem to have been accepted by the Jerusalem Church.[23] The fact that when he begins his ministry his mother doubts his sanity and tries to take him home is an indication that she has not had heard the story! But what is not history is poetry. A new age has begun, and through this birth God has entered into the world. As Richard Crashaw so wonderfully puts it,

> Welcome, all wonders in one sight!
> Eternity shut up in a span!
> Summer in winter, day in night!
> Heaven in earth, and God in man!
> Great little One! whose all-embracing birth
> Lifts earth to heaven, stoops heaven to earth.[24]

The power of these Nativity stories is their gift to our imagination. Poets, hymnwriters, artists, preachers, junior church teachers, and parents all can use them.

## THE CRUCIFIED GOD

Above all there are two Jesus stories which go the heart of life's meaning—crucifixion and resurrection. The first is without question a historical fact—whatever you would make up it would hardly be this. Crucifixion

---

22. L'Engle, *Cry Like a Bell*, 58.
23. Goulder, *Missions*, 109f.
24. Batchelor, *Christian Poetry Collection*, 282.

was a lingering death. People might take days to die, tortured by thirst, tormented by flies. The Romans always did it as publicly as possible, by a city gate or along the main roads, so that everyone could see exactly what happened if you defied Rome. Christianity's founder, the one in whom we see the human face of God, was an obscure nobody who died a humiliating death, abandoned by almost everyone. He is credibly recorded as dying in something like despair—"My God, my God, why have you forsaken me?" (Mark 15:34). As an image of God, it is extraordinarily unlikely. As John Buchanan puts it, "Weakness, suffering, dying as a victim at the hands of the state—those are not terms we ordinarily use to discuss God."[25] Normally we think of God as omnipotent, omniscient, and omnibenevolent. It is hard to see that in a broken man crying out in the face of a fate he can't understand and the nonchalant indifference of the Romans who snuff out his life. If this is how we see God, what can it possibly mean for faith?

In all honesty our natural instinct is to look away and find more congenial ways of understanding God. A triumphant Christ, Christ the King, Christ Pantocrator, the ruler of the universe, or Christ the teacher. We prefer to take the body off the cross, make it all beautiful and aesthetically pleasing. At the very least have a nice sunset to give the cross a pleasing background. On the front of his *Isenheim Altarpiece*, Mathias Grünewald painted an image of Christ contorted in pain, thorns sticking out of his deathly grey skin, covered in wounds from being beaten. By contrast Salvador Dalí, in his *Christ of Saint John of the Cross* sought the opposite effect. He wrote,

> I want to paint a Christ that is a painting with more beauty and joy than have ever been painted before. I want to paint a Christ that is the absolute opposite of Grünewald's materialistic savagely anti-mystical one.[26]

This is a misconception of 'Christ in divine glory'—by taking away the bloody truth it loses the stark reality which makes the event so distinctive. It reminds me of those who want to sing of Jesus, "How beautiful you are"—moving on from the historical to the mystical. One might argue that the Gospel of John does exactly this, moving away from the abandonment and desolation of Mark to a more triumphal view of the cross, so there is good biblical precedence for this. But the more you distance yourself from

---

25. Buchanan, "No Story So Divine."
26. Dalí, *Unspeakable Confessions of Salvador Dalí*, 217.

the broken, bloodied Christ the greater the danger that the scandal of the cross, "a stumbling block to Jews and foolishness to Gentiles" (1 Cor 1:23), is replaced by something more conventional and congenial—a successful Christ who will show us how to get what we want and enjoy what we get. This it must be admitted may have more popular appeal than a Christ, who "hath no form nor comeliness; and when we shall see him, there is no beauty that we should desire him" (Isa 53:2).

Personally, one of the things I like to do by way of preparation for Holy Week and Easter is to spend some time listening to music. Often great music can go deeper than any words a preacher might use. So, I listen to Bach's Passion music. The words and the music come together in my head.

> O Sacred Head sore wounded
> With grief and shame weighed down . . .
>
> What language shall I borrow
> To thank thee, dearest friend.[27]

Or Handel's Messiah: "He was despised and rejected of men, a man of sorrows, and acquainted with grief." I read Mark's account of the passion: "When it was noon, darkness came over the whole land" (Mark 15:33). I love the service of Tenebrae, as the passion is read so the candles are extinguished until finally there is the real pain of the Christ being snuffed out and we go on our way silently into the darkness.

I see three things in this darkness. Firstly, if a crucified man is the supreme image of God, then our whole value system is overturned. As Tom Holland says, "It is the audacity of it—the audacity of finding in a twisted and defeated corpse the glory of the creator of the universe."[28] If God is supremely found among the rejected and despised then Matthew 25 really is at the heart of the gospel, "in as much as you did unto the least of these my brothers and sisters." As Marty Haugen puts it,

> Here the outcast and the stranger
> bear the image of God's face.[29]

The imperative is that in serving those in need we are closer to God than when with the powerful. Mother Theresa was closer to God when rescuing beggars from the street than when hobnobbing with the Pope or

---

27. United Reformed Church, *Rejoice and Sing*, 220.
28. *Spectator*, Apr 20, 2019.
29. Methodist Church, *Singing the Faith*, 409.

borrowing a corrupt millionaire's private jet. God's will runs in the direction of equality.

One need hardly say this is not our world as we know it. William Willimon remembers being told by William Sloane Coffin not to worry too much about his Holy Week sermon. "Anybody can preach on Good Friday," he said. "Hell, read the newspaper!"[30] In South Africa a man falls into a drainage channel by the side of the roadside: "White man down," someone shouts. In the US George Floyd is killed by a police officer, who kneels on the neck of the helpless man who is begging "I can't breathe." Such cases are in the context of a world of structural injustice and vast economic inequalities. The twenty-two richest men in the world have more wealth than all 325 million women in Africa. According to UNICEF, twenty-two thousand children die each day due to poverty. Every year over half a million people are trafficked across international borders, up to 50 percent of them minors. The Home Office estimates that there are up to four thousand victims of trafficking for sexual exploitation in the UK at any one time. Jim Wallis tells how when he moved to Washington, he joined with neighbors to start a simple food line on Saturday mornings, where many people lined up just twenty blocks from the White House to get a big bag of groceries that would get their families through the week. Before they opened the door on one occasion Mary Glover, a Pentecostal woman, prayed,

> Thank you, Lord, for waking me up this morning; that the walls of my room were not the walls of my grave, and my bed was not my cooling board. Lord, we know that you will be coming through this line today, so Lord, help us to treat you well—help us to treat you well. Amen.[31]

That is part of the challenge and demand of a crucified saviour. Thomas Traherne makes the point more poetically:

> O Christ, I see thy cross of thorns in every eye, thy bleeding naked wounded body in every soul, thy death lived in every memory. Thy crucified person is embalmed in every affliction, thy pierced feet are bathed in everyone's tears.[32]

---

30. *Christian Century*, Mar 24, 2021.
31. *Sojourners*, Mar 2, 2017.
32. Traherne, *Centuries of Meditations*, 86.

I cannot claim to live this out at all adequately. Nor of course does the church. But it's a challenge and an inspiration. As a moral imperative it is hugely powerful. At the heart of the Christian life is an obligation to the vulnerable, to others. It judges us, inspires us, and sometimes at least inspires us to action.

Then secondly, the crucifixion says something about God and suffering. Wonderful as life often is, pain and suffering are inescapable. I once went on a Methodist Quiet Day to a retreat center in the Surrey Hills. Inevitably they never stopped talking. When I could, I slipped away for a walk. I thought I could look up at the hills, feel the beauty of nature, and soak up the atmosphere. Instead on the path were the bloody, torn remains of some half-eaten animal. It was unedifying, a reminder of the brutality and sometimes sheer anguish of life. We are part of a world in which innocent people suffer, suicide bombers kill, precious young soldiers die, tests come back positive, old age can be filled with indignity, relationships sour and die. A world, incidentally, which will ultimately be destroyed, utterly wiping out all forms of life—if we have not done that ourselves long before. That a man of unquestionable goodness dies in the horror of painful execution and humiliation fits exactly this waste of life.

Trying to make any sense of a belief in a God of love in this context is difficult—and I shall return to this again. But at least one thing one can say now is that Christians have seen God in that moment of crucifixion. The cross is a symbol of a God we meet in suffering. This is a very dangerous idea. It can lead to believing that suffering is a gift of God, monks and nuns whipping themselves, or a sadomasochist cult of suffering as in Mel Gibson's *The Passion of the Christ* with its relentless portrayal of violence and torture beyond anything in the Gospels. It can lead to the bizarre and morally dubious theory that Jesus must suffer and die as the price for God forgiving us, which seems to find its origin in the belief that blood sacrifice is necessary to appease a deity. As one extremely popular hymn puts it,

> Till on that cross as Jesus died,
> The wrath of God was satisfied.[33]

Father, forgive them, for they know not what they sing. Jesus died for standing up to empire, not to satisfy the blood lust of a morally crazed God. There are better ways of understanding the cross than this, as anyone who has read the parable of the Prodigal Son would know—not a God of wrath

---

33. *Songs of Fellowship*, No. 780.

but a God whose justice is always tempered by love, a God who is more like a parent, a God whose dealing with wayward children is more like a loving mother or father. This is the God we see at Calvary, a God whose love can be met even in suffering. As Julian of Norwich said in the century of Europe's most deadly plague:

> If there be anywhere on earth a lover of God who is always kept safe from falling, I know nothing of it—for it was not shown me. But this was shown: that in falling and rising again, we are always held close in one love.[34]

As a minister I know perfectly well that this is not a universal experience. There are people who have no awareness of God in suffering. As we learned after her death Mother Theresa experienced the absence of God, something she never revealed in life. "I spoke as if my very heart was in love with God—tender, personal love," she wrote to one adviser. "If you were (there), you would have said, 'What hypocrisy.'" One may wonder whether Jesus had any awareness of God as he died—very possibly not. But the cross is a sign of hope, that even in the darkest, even most hopeless place God's love is present and there is hope. "Yea, though I walk through the valley of the shadow of death, I will fear no evil: for thou art with me" (Ps 23:6). Even there God can bring good from evil, death gives life. In this sense the cross is a hugely positive and powerful symbol.

Thirdly, the cross is a symbol of God's love. The simple fact is that Jesus had no need to be there. I believe he knew where events were leading and went ahead because this was how redemption could take place. But whether he could see that far ahead or not, he was still there when he need not have been. He died still forgiving. Put simply it is love that brings him to the cross, a giving of himself for others. Some people look at Jesus and ask, "Is he like God?" I find it more productive to do it the other way round, to look at the cross and ask what it means if God is like that. Trying to cope with life, this is where we gain a world to live in. Speaking of the church Marty Haugen writes,

> Here the cross shall stand as witness
> and as symbol of God's grace.[35]

It does for me. At one point in my life, I found myself in a personal crisis which left me nearly broken by pain. I went into a religious bookshop

---

34. Friedrich, "Terrible Work."
35. Methodist Church, *Singing the Faith*, 409.

in Birmingham and bought a cross which I put on the wall above my desk in my study. It said to me, nothing in life can separate you from God's love. God loves you like that. In the moments in life when you feel lost in the darkness God is there with you. Forty years on it is still there and I can see it every time I look up from my computer. Then as now I need it.

## RESURRECTION

Powerful as the cross is for Christian faith, if there was no counter-balancing, more hopeful, story to go with it, this would lead to a rather bleak view of faith, just as it would have been bleak for the disciples had the cross been the last word on Jesus. But along with the symbol of the cross goes the story of resurrection, of Jesus' triumph over death and light overcoming the darkness. The joining of the two together gives both realism and potency. The cross faces the stark reality of life's pain, the resurrection witnesses to hope. Suffering is inseparable from life, but Christ is risen, sin is overcome, darkness gives way to light, love has proved stronger. You can see it in the way we date Easter on the first Sunday after the spring equinox, after which the days are longer than the night. So the whole cosmos welcomes Christ's victory.

All this is dependent on a historical event—the raising of Jesus from the dead. But it is more than that—it is a story that catches the human hope for life and of love's victory. That is why for me as a preacher Easter Sunday is the best day of the year. On one occasion I was in Southampton Hospital for a month with a broken leg after a traffic accident, but I was determined that if it was humanly possible, I would be back in the pulpit by Easter Sunday—which with the aid of a walking stick I was. Everything hinges on what actually happened then. If Jesus' life ended in abandonment and pain then as powerful a symbol of God's love as the cross is, it would not be credible to claim that love is at the heart of life. Paul puts it more precisely: "If Christ has not been raised, your faith is futile" (1 Cor 15:17).

Historically it is impossible to prove what happened on the first Easter. Peter Gomes says that Easter turns the preacher into a lawyer examining the evidence, looking at each piece to prove the case. But this is a pointless exercise. A. J. M. Wedderburn is more honest about it than some Christian preachers are. "Very little can be verified historically above and beyond the disciples' faith: something, a mysterious something, happened to them, but further than that we cannot penetrate."[36] Was there an empty tomb? Who was the first resurrection witness? Was the first resurrection experience in Jerusalem or Galilee? Was the resurrection physical? On each of these questions the traditional answer may be right—but we cannot be certain that it is. On Easter Sunday no preacher in their senses tries to prove exactly what happened—how can we know?

In fact, an obsession with the facts may not be helpful. As Sherlock Holmes once said: "One in pursuit of a criminal should not pay too much attention to evidence, Watson, it gets in the way." I preach most years on John's beautiful story of Mary mistaking Jesus for the gardener. What history, if any, lies behind it I cannot be certain, and I am not going to use valuable preaching time offering the possibilities. The stories are hugely evocative and bring Easter alive.

> Simple sentences leap out
> of the Big Black Book
> like friends:
> 'Supposing him to be the gardener'
> 'Did not our hearts burn within us?'
> 'Come and have breakfast-'
> Divine ends.[37]

I would not wish to have to seek their actual origins. So much of the Bible is poetry, myths, symbols, parables, or stories where the actual history is impossible to determine with any certainty, that a constant search for what actually happened often misses the point. We cannot and should not try to draw too absolute a distinction between them. Of course, we may (and sometimes should) conclude the stories we hear are untrue or the symbols not relevant to us. But mostly we rightly let the stories speak to us, understanding that the language of God is more poetry than dissection.

When it comes to the resurrection this does, however, have to be a symbol rooted in fact. One of the most challenging Easter Poems is John Updike's *Seven Stanzas at Easter*. He is rightly emphatic:

> Make no mistake: if He rose at all
> it was as His body....
> It was not as the flowers,

---

36. Wedderburn, *Beyond Resurrection*, 89. "Die shall I in order to live. Rise again, yes, rise again, will you, my heart, in an instant! That for which you suffered, to God will it lead you!"

37. Harries, *Hearing God in Poetry*, 178

> each soft Spring recurrent;
> it was not as His Spirit in the mouths and fuddled eyes of the
> eleven apostles;
> it was as His Flesh: ours.[38]

The resurrection has to be real to carry the weight. If this is the moment when you know that love is stronger than death and goodness than evil, something amazing has to have happened. I may not be able to pin it down, but it has to be real. If you make the resurrection a weak metaphor based on the fact that flowers come out in the spring, or that people who have been depressed can feel hope again, then it trivializes the resurrection into a nothing. When I look at the bloody slaughter in Ukraine, I need more than that, if I am going to still say that Easter shows that the arc of history bends towards justice. The resurrection has to be the action of God, not just our response to events. But then Updike spoils it for me:

> Make no mistake: if he rose at all
> It was as His body;
> If the cell's dissolution did not reverse, the molecule reknit,
> The amino acids rekindle . . .
> The same hinged thumbs and toes
> The same valved heart
> That—pierced—died, withered, paused, and then regathered.[39]

In other words, death simply goes into reverse, the resurrection is about a reanimated corpse. This makes no sense at all. How do you credibly postulate a reanimated body which can materialize and dematerialize in differing localities at will? Nor is it biblical. There is no consistency in the New Testament about the nature of the resurrection experiences but certainly Paul (whose own Damascus Road experience was clearly spiritual) is dismissive of amino acids rekindling. "Flesh and blood cannot inherit the Kingdom of God" (1 Cor 15:50). As David Jenkins says, "Obviously he thinks it is stupid to be literal minded about physical bodies when thinking, and hoping, about the Resurrection."[40] It is well to remember, as David Bentley Hart reminds us, that, to the authors of scripture, the spiritual was *more real* than the physical. "Spirit was something subtler but also

---

38. Batchelor, *Christian Poetry Collection*, 317.
39. Batchelor, *Christian Poetry Collection*, 317.
40. Jenkins and Jenkins, *Free to Believe*, 44.

stronger, more vital, more glorious than the worldly elements of a coarse corruptible body compounded of earthly soul and material flesh."[41]

Exactly what happened on Easter Day is not for us to know. Historically it is clear there was a dramatic change in the lives of the disciples which they attributed to a meeting with the risen Christ. But we certainly cannot prove what happened. However early we run to the tomb we will find he is not there to view, and we shall come away as uncertain as the disciples did. If the resurrection makes sense to us, it can only be because our own experience gives credence to it. Rowan Williams says it well: "The believer's life is a testimony to the risen-ness of Jesus: he or she demonstrates that Jesus is not dead by living a life in which Jesus is the never-failing source of affirmation, challenge, enrichment, and enlargement."[42] I would put it more inclusively. The resurrection is credible if we find in our experience in God a power which forgives, restores, and renews, a transfiguring presence in a world fraught with absences. You catch the feel of it in Norman Adams's stations of the cross which, in the last one, is bursting into flower with a new life after death. We too can rise with Christ, it promises, to a new life where death has been defeated.

Resurrection is not a one-off event which we look for in the past. Resurrection is the victory of life over death, love over hate. Paul Tillich puts it powerfully:

> Death is given power over everything finite . . . But death is given no power over love. Love is stronger. It creates something new out of the destruction caused by death. It bears everything and overcomes everything. It rescues life from death. It rescues each of us, for love is stronger than death.[43]

This has absolutely nothing to do with amino acids. But it is the promise that life can be lived in the conviction that love goes to the heart of it and is more powerful than anything life can throw at us.

Gustav Mahler said of his Second Symphony ("Resurrection") that he was asking the big questions: "What did you live for? Why did you suffer? Is it all only a vast terrifying joke?"[44] The music is full of menacing uncertainty and discordant noise; it is about death and life, with a huge orchestra and full of intensity. In the third movement the music lets out a scream—sometimes

---

41. *Church Life Journal*, Jul 22, 2018.
42. Williams, *Resurrection*, 55.
43. Tillich, *Boundaries of Our Being*, 280–81.
44. Mahler, *Selected Letters of Gustav Mahler*, 180.

called the death shriek. The chaos of life is too much, and we hear it. The scream almost collapses the orchestral sound. But then in the great finale the chorus refutes the turmoil. The suffering is not pointless. "Die shall I in order to live. Rise again, yes, rise again, will you, my heart, in an instant! That for which you suffered, to God will it lead you!" Love is the climax of all. Jim Friedrich tells how he first heard the symphony from the third row of the Los Angeles Philharmonic with Zubin Mehta and Jessye Norman. It ended in a gigantic wave of sound:

> In the emotionally charged silence which followed the Philharmonic's inspired performance, no one dared clap or even whisper. Mehta kept his arms high and extended, seemingly frozen in his final gesture, for a very long thirty seconds, forbidding us to drown out "the note that is no more" with the harshness of applause. Norman's eyes welled up. Some of the orchestra wiped away tears. It was the closest I've come to eternity. At last, very slowly, Mehta lowered his arms. When they finally reached his side, his shoulders relaxed, and we were all released back into time. We rose to our feet and thundered our joy. Yes, that sublime moment had kept futility at bay. More than that, it had carried us to God.[45]

The resurrection is the triumphant yes to life.

## JESUS—THE CHURCH'S STORY

A letter published in the *Times* on May 17, 2014, recorded an incident involving Enoch Powell:

> Sir, Enoch Powell once attended a county fete and was amused to see an "Enoch Powell lookalike" competition. On the spur of the moment (and having a much greater sense of humour than he was usually credited with) he entered, incognito. He came third. (John Hurdley, Highclere, Hants).

If the task of the church is to incarnate the life of Christ one suspects the resemblance will be no more obviously apparent. Historically in terms of origin it may be the case that "the Church's one foundation is Jesus Christ her Lord," but it would not be wise to assume with any particular church, at any particular moment in history, that this is actually the case. Sometimes

---

45. *Religious Imaginer*, Sep 12, 2015.

the church reflects the world or authority or nationalism more than the Galilean carpenter.

Nonetheless the Church lives by and with the story of Jesus. If we know Jesus today it is through the church. In it the scriptures are read, and the story is remembered. Throughout the Christian year the liturgy follows the life story of Jesus, interspersed with teaching, music, reflections, and prayer. Its power and subversive nature keep on breaking through. In so doing it dramatizes the great issues of life and death in a way which opens up their place in our own lives. There's an interesting little story in the Gospel of John. Two men are standing with John the Baptist when Jesus walks by. "Look," John says. "Look, the Lamb of God. He's what we're all looking for." You might regard that as a kind of proto-church. What happened there was in essence what happened to me at Shrub End Congregational Church and in the Christian Association in Hull. In the story the men leave John and start to follow Jesus. "What are you looking for?" he asks. Later, Andrew, one of the two, brings his brother Peter. Whatever happened that day changed Andrew forever and Peter too—and, through them, the history of the world. They found something big enough to commit their lives to. Someone who made God real and so made everything seem to matter more. It still happens today.

# 5

# "WHAT LIFE HAVE YOU IF YOU HAVE NOT LIFE TOGETHER?"

NOT FAR AWAY FROM where I lived in Swindon is one of England's oldest and most spectacular sacred spaces—the Avebury stone circles. It is the largest megalithic stone circle in the world, an outer ring with around one hundred megaliths, a huge bank and ditch, two smaller circles, and at least two avenues of standing stones. Unlike Stonehenge there is open access and the sheer size of it means that despite the hordes of tourists you can often still feel the awe of it. It developed in stages over a thousand years but the great henge dates from around 2600 to 2500 BC. Coming across it in 1649 John Aubrey claimed it to "exceed Stonehenge as a cathedral does a parish Church," which is what I feel myself. Its purpose is obscure, though the presence of human bones may indicate funerary rites. One archaeologist has suggested that people gathered "to appease the malevolent powers of nature" that threatened their existence, such as the winter cold, death, and disease. But, as Barry Cunliffe says, "the possibilities for speculation are endless."[1] Certainly people came to worship and indeed still do. Sacred spaces take their meaning not just from the stones but from the people who worshiped there, their hopes and beliefs and fears.

In my time at Swindon I too worshiped at Avebury, actually in the stone circle. Near the center of the monument was Avebury United Reformed Church, where I led worship on a number of occasions, always feeling the strangeness of leading worship only thirty-five meters from the

---

1. Cunliffe, *Britain Begins*, 183.

largest megalith in the complex. A meeting house was built here in 1707 when the Five Mile Act prohibited ejected Nonconformist Ministers taking services within five miles of their former church. Taking advantage of what was available they built it of sarsen stone from the henge. At the center of its life as minister from 1972 to 1999 was the Rev. Bert Jones, who combined his ministry with working for British Telecom. He was very much a country man and an indefatigable promoter of his little congregation. In 1979, after he had taken a funeral service for one of them, Grace Kersley wrote to thank him.

> Dear Mr. Jones,
>
> It was inspiring to be at Aunt Nellie's funeral service yesterday, and to know she is now "Singing the praises of JESUS her Good Shepherd within His House for ever." How she loved to sing His praises in His House at Avebury. Her life was centred there, everything she did was related to carrying on the ministry of the Church. The flowers she grew in her garden were for the Church, the time she spent cleaning the Church, weeding the path, trimming the oil lamps (some years ago), seeing the oil heaters were working properly and the church was as warm as she could possibly make it, this was her life. She entertained the visiting preachers to tea for as long as she was able, and then made sure they had a flask of tea in the church when the days for having them to her home were over.[2]

Churches are not just buildings, or architecture or sacred spaces. They are Auntie Nellie and Bert Jones and the people who worship there.

Wrong in what they denied, the Puritans were right in what they affirmed. A church is not a building but people. It is a community who share worship, life, and mission. When Paul speaks of the church it is always this community of shared discipleship he has in mind, never a building. It finds beautiful expression in Corinthians where the church is compared to a body where everyone has their part to play. "For just as the body is one and has many members, and all the members of the body, though many, are one body, so it is with Christ" (1 Cor 12:12). It is to be a community in which all are valued and accepted in an inclusive love. "If one member suffers, all suffer" (1 Cor 12:26). You may start with the building, it may be the most visible expression of religious faith, but the community who gather there matters more.

2. "History of Avebury Congregational Chapel."

## "WHAT LIFE HAVE YOU IF YOU HAVE NOT LIFE TOGETHER?"

Certainly, that has been true for me. The experience of sacred space is a core part of my religious experience, but it is not where my faith began, nor has it ever been its most important element. My faith began with me growing up in a faith community. It had not a little to do with the fact that my mother was a Congregationalist, and her mother before her a Congregationalist! Christian faith and being part of a community are inexplicably linked together. The East Anglian churches in which I grew up had very little to offer to me as a young person—at that point my faith was nurtured more by books than anything else. But all that changed when I went to university at Hull in 1966. Here were people of my own age who shared my searching faith. The Congregational-Presbyterian Society was tiny, but I also joined the much stronger Methodist Society and by my second year was chair of the ecumenical Christian Association. Much of my life centered around it. There were bread-and-cheese lunches at the Anglican and Catholic chaplaincies and in the office of Fred Fletcher, the Quaker chaplain. There were discussion groups, meetings, worship, and parties. It was wonderfully ecumenical, introducing me to wider vistas than my own background of placid East Anglian Congregationalism could offer.

It was the time of John Robinson's *Honest to God*, the New Reformation, ecumenical vision, and Martin Luther King marching for racial justice. The optimism of those days is now difficult to recapture. Did the World Conference on Church and Society meeting at Geneva in 1966 actually say, "We know that God appears to have set no limits to what may be achieved by our generation?"[3] When the Beatles could confidently assure us that life was getting better and Bob Dylan that the times were changing.

When President Kennedy said, "Never before has man had such capacity to control his own environment, to end thirst and hunger, to conquer poverty and disease, to banish illiteracy and massive human misery,"[4] it was axiomatic that this was true. Everything I did at university seemed to have Simon and Garfunkel as background music and the film *The Graduate* crystallized the mood that the young needed to strike out in new directions from the stuffy old world that went before. When it came to the church it seemed obvious that the old denominational landscape had little relevance to a post-God modern world, and that the only way we could really hope serve the present age was together. It was prophetic voices like Dietrich Bonhoeffer who put this most powerfully, and it was this which

---

3. Hastings, *Oliver Tomkins*, 128.
4. Kennedy, "Address before the 18th General Assembly."

led the Nottingham Conference in 1964 to a commitment to church unity by 1980—for the sake of the world. It was this which was the great impetus to the creation of the United Reformed Church. Utopian as much of it in retrospect was, it gave me commitments which have lasted a lifetime.

All of this for me was rooted in the experience of being part of the student Christian community. Through it I made friends, I shared worship and was influenced by ideas. Like all good communities it sometimes worked as a marriage mart—Catholics married Methodists, Anglicans married Congregationalists, and I married a local Methodist preacher who had been chairman (!) of the Christian Association the year before me. Quite a few, like me, ended up being ordained or going to lifetimes of significant service to the church. The even then obviously formidably intelligent Eamon Duffy became Britain's foremost Catholic historian and David Gamble became president of the Methodist Conference.

All this is rooted in the fundamentals of human nature. We are who we are because of others. The homes we grow up in, the teachers who taught us, the people who helped us, and those who shared hopes and dreams with us. None of us is a self-made woman or man. We carry with us generations of people before us who help make us who we are. Our beliefs bear the impact of the generation in which we lived, and the traditions we've inherited, and the people we've lived with. Unsurprisingly this is true of our faith as well. The South African idea of *ubuntu* takes us to the heart of what Christianity is all about. It means "I am because you are." Archbishop Desmond Tutu says, "[It] means my humanity is caught up, is inextricably bound up, in theirs. We belong in a bundle of life. We say, 'a person is a person through other people.' It is not 'I think therefore I am.' It says rather: 'I am human because I belong. I participate, I share.'"[5] Or, if you prefer T.S. Eliot,

> What life have you if you have not life together?
> There is no life that is not in community,
> And no community not lived in praise of GOD.[6]

---

5. Tutu, *No Future without Forgiveness*, 34–36.
6. Eliot, *Complete Poems and Plays*, 152.

"WHAT LIFE HAVE YOU IF YOU HAVE NOT LIFE TOGETHER?"

## A JESUS-CENTERED COMMUNITY SHARING THE LOVE OF GOD

The belief that faith is lived out in community is part of the basic perception of Jesus. He himself lived his life within the formal structures of religion, the synagogue, the temple. And he clearly intended to gather a new community to continue his work. It would be naïve to imagine that Jesus intended anything like the institutional church as we know it. As James Dunn says, "By 'church' it is hard to avoid the idea of the church as it has been known down through the centuries—the Churches of Eastern Orthodoxy, the Church of Rome, the Churches of Protestantism . . . and presumably Jesus did not envisage all of that."[7] A good bit of what churches have thought utterly vital would no doubt have left him either mystified or appalled. Auntie Nellie was certainly not on his radar nor indeed the Papacy or the Ecumenical Patriarch. It is unlikely he had any idea of the great sweep of history ahead at all.

But Jesus was not an individualist. He gathered a community around him to be the catalyst for the coming of the kingdom. "Where two or three are gathered together in my name," says Jesus, "I am there among them" (Matt 18:20). One might justifiably be cautious about the historicity of "You are Peter, and on this rock, I will build my church" (Matt 16:18). The word "church" has a distinctively anachronistic sound to it and looks as if it was fashioned by the church to make a point about its own authority. But Jesus did intend to leave behind followers, a movement, a company of men and women and children. As Dunn says, his vision of discipleship was of "a community organised to support missionaries reaching out to others with evangelistic urgency and to maintain a witness by the very quality of their community life."[8] Jesus carefully formed this community, taught them, nurtured them, loved them, and prepared them to carry on after he was gone. They were to embody the good news of God's love in the world just as he had done and to love one another and the world with the same passion he had.

At Pentecost the community was renewed and became the infant church. In Acts 2 the description of the early Church begins. "All who believed were together" (Acts 2:44). Christianity is faith lived with others in community. This is what John Wesley saw when he wrote, "the Gospel

---

7. Dunn, *Discipleship*, 93.
8. Dunn, *Discipleship*, 115.

of Christ knows of no religion but social; no holiness but social holiness."[9] As Wesley said,

> it is only when we are *knit together*, that we *have Nourishment from Him, and increase with the Increase of GOD*. Neither is there any time, when the weakest Member can say to the strongest, or the strongest to the weakest, "*I have no need of Thee.*"[10]

## THE REALITY OF CHURCH

At this point reality needs to intrude. Anyone who imagines that churches always live up to this is in for a severe disappointment. I remember when my sister moved to Coventry, going with her to try one of the local churches. We went as a fairly large family group. After the service we sat there for several minutes, but no one spoke to us. We made our way out—still no one spoke. It can be worse than that. Paul only reminds the Corinthians that the church is to be a loving community because the reality was quite otherwise. Sometimes religion can be a façade for self-righteousness, personal ambition, or narrow pettiness.

This has been very visibly illustrated by the bitterness and divisiveness that has not infrequently been part of the debate about human sexuality in the church. When the Lambeth Conference in 1998 gave backing to an anti-gay resolution, Andrew Brown and Linda Woodhead commented, "What was actually more shocking was the vanity, the naked politicking between clerical camps, and the absence of any suggestion of the things that might make going to church worthwhile."[11] Similar examples abound. When Gene Robinson was consecrated as the first openly gay bishop in the Episcopal Church in the US, he felt it necessary to wear a bulletproof vest because of the number of death threats he had received.[12] In her *Leaving Church* Barbara Brown Taylor gives a searingly honest account of her personal life story leading up to her leaving the church's ministry. As rector of Grace-Calvary Episcopal Church at Clarkesville, Georgia, she found herself trying to deal with increasingly bitter debates as the congregation struggled with the issue. "As a general rule, I would say that human beings never behave

---

9. Wesley and Wesley, *Hymns and Sacred Poems*, 8.
10. Wesley, *Works*, 592.
11. Brown and Woodhead, *That Was the Church that Was*, 155–6.
12. *Guardian*, Nov 7, 2010.

more badly toward one another than when they believe they are protecting God."[13] Iain McDonald, who was the first openly gay person to be accepted for ordination training in the URC, tells how one West Country URC, on learning of his sexuality, banned him from both preaching and playing the organ. Indeed, one of the elders demanded the organ be rededicated as it had been contaminated!

Though extreme this is not a one-off. According to Justin Welby the Church of England is "still deeply institutionally racist."[14] No one should make light of this. Nonetheless if realism involves recognizing the pretensions and failures of the church it also recognizes that this is to be expected of any human organization. As Eugene Peterson observes, "Community is intricate and complex. Living in community as a people of God is inherently messy. A congregation consists of many people of various moods, ideas, needs, experiences . . . It is not easy, and it is not simple."[15] Inevitably community life is fragmentary and frustrating, but that does not mean we can live the life we want without it. Without the community I could not be a Christian in any meaningful sense.

Literature offers one way of seeing, often in unintended ways, the reality of church life. I am a devotee of the English provincial novel expressed in the great tradition of Jane Austen, Anthony Trollope, Thomas Hardy, George Eliot, and Mrs. Gaskell. These only occasionally center on religious issues. Even in Trollope's *Barchester* novels of clerical life the real center of interest is more often who marries who and who gets what job! But as observers of their time they picture some of the reality of church life.

In the novels social and community life unmistakably centers around the churches. People of all sorts and social classes attend. Sermons are enjoyed or endured. "When I married Humphrey," said Mrs. Cadwallader in *Middlemarch*, "I made up my mind to like sermons, and I set out by liking the end very much. That soon spread to the middle and the beginning because I couldn't have the end without them."[16] Weddings are celebrated and children baptized. Thomas Hardy refers to,

> Baptisms, burials, doctorings, conjugal counsel-
> all the whatnots asked of a rural parson.[17]

---

13. Taylor, *Leaving Church*, 106.
14. BBC News, Feb 12, 2020.
15. *Christian Century*, Feb 12, 2008.
16. Eliot, *Middlemarch*, 359.
17. Hardy, *Selected Poetry*, 162–63.

Charity is dispensed to the poor. Cathedral choirs provide superb music and hymn singing is enjoyed. Motives for church attendance are mixed. In the TV version of *Cranford*, Dr. Harrison, on being asked why he is hurrying to church when he not very religious, replies, "I am a doctor in this community, I have connections to maintain!"[18] I am reminded that Denis Healey walked a mile to attend Utley Congregational Church because his father "felt this ritual would commend him to Mrs. Craven Laycock, the grand old lady Congregationalist who was Chairman of his Education Committee."[19] But churchgoing is not always a formality. In *Pride and Prejudice*, Mr. Darcy is to be found not only in church on Sunday but also on occasions such as Good Friday where social form does not require his attendance.

The clergy are far from ideal. "I don't know that clergymen are so much better than other men,"[20] says the wife of Trollope's Archdeacon Grantly. He is the perfect example of this undoubted truth. Described by Trollope as "a proud, wistful, worldly man," he is very aware of money, position, and the good things of life. Others are equally problematic. Given a choice it is difficult to be certain whether being married to Mr. Collins or the Rev. Obadiah Slope would be a worse fate. But the novels also celebrate clerical virtue, found in characters like Edmund Bertram of *Mansfield Park* and Dr. Shirley in *Persuasion* or Trollope's Septimus Harding. Some clergymen, like George Eliot's Mr. Farebrother in *Middlemarch*, are influential in the community and attractively embody the Christian values of love, generosity, and acceptance. All of this reflects the actual moral muddle of clergy life which includes the pastorally dedicated and the self-obsessed, the energetic and the lazy, those who are deeply concerned for others and the Methodist minister I know who was fined for drunken driving, and the one whose eyes, rather improbably, grew bright at the thought of being Methodist chair of district.

As in real life, so to these authors doubt and faith often come mixed. Jane Austen came from the reasonable world of eighteenth-century Anglicanism and is secure in her faith, though clearly not uncritical. She knows its vices. Mary Crawford in *Mansfield Park* can say, "A clergyman has nothing to do but be slovenly and selfish—read the newspaper, watch the weather, and quarrel with his wife. His curate does all the work, and

---

18. *Cranford*, "August 1842," aired May 4, 2008. TV episode.
19. Healey, *Time of My Life*, 7.
20. Trollope, *Barchester Towers*, 418.

the business of his own life is to dine."[21] But she knows this is not the whole truth. Edmund's reply, "There are such clergymen, no doubt, but I think they are not so common as to justify . . . esteeming it their general character,"[22] is reflected in her picture of the clergy. She herself clearly upholds the Christian virtues of goodness, truth, charity, prudence, and honor, and these are the qualities she values in her characters. It is such inner virtues which produce character. She wasn't a vicar's daughter for nothing.

Later, as the "sea of faith" ebbs, the turmoil is reflected in the literature. In the Unitarian Mrs. Gaskell's *North and South* Mr. Hale resigns as a vicar because of growing doubt as to the traditional doctrines of the church. George Eliot too experienced the struggle for faith. Her own early evangelicalism ebbed away and translating David Strauss's *Life of Jesus* which revealed the mythic elements in the Christian story, left her reeling—"Strauss sick," she called it, feeling that she had lost part of herself. But her Christianity had gone deep and remained part of her. She remains concerned with what Ronald Thiemann calls the "humble sublime" working out religious ideas in a secular context. Her characters grew through suffering, she had a passion for righteousness, a reverence for life and a sense that to gain your life you had to be willing to lose it. Unlike most Victorian novelists she could even find good in Nonconformity. Dinah Morris's passionate Methodist faith shines out in *Adam Bede*, and her picture of Methodism is of ordinary people finding:

> a faith which linked their thoughts with the past, lifted their imagination above the sordid details of their narrow lives, and suffused their souls with the sense of a pitying, loving, infinite presence.[23]

This is without doubt idealized but not entirely untrue.

There is a realism about this which reflects church life perhaps just as well (or even better) than many pious justifications for it. It realistically shows that for great sections of society the church was part of the warp and weft of community life—deeply imperfect, full of very ambiguous people, but shaping lives, giving rituals that build meaning, and in some senses at least a moral community. Without it the novels would be the poorer, and so would the lives of the people. For better or for worse the church was a

---

21. Austen, *Mansfield Park*, 137.
22. Austen, *Mansfield Park*, 137.
23. Eliot, *Adam Bede*, 81–82.

hugely significant factor not simply in faith formation but in the life of the whole community.

My own experience reflects all this. My first church, for example, was small with around 120 members and a church community of probably no more than 200. That enabled me to visit most of the homes around once a year. It meant that if anyone was in hospital I would expect to be there within a day or so and to return every week until they were discharged. If any new person came, I would hope to visit them at home once they had established a pattern of attendance. At Christmas I would take presents round to all the elderly. Sometimes I would look in on those who were not in any way part of the church but who seemed to appreciate a visit. I would visit the Women's Fellowship most weeks and look in at the mothers and babies group or the young adults. When someone died, I would visit and usually return with decreasing frequency in the weeks ahead. Quite often I had people around to the manse for a not very well-cooked dinner. It may have helped that I was single and did not have a wife or children to worry about, but this did not mean that I did not have the time to be active in the community, or to take a day off to watch cricket when the opportunity arose. This would no doubt have been impossible with a larger congregation, or a multiple church pastorate, but it was entirely feasible with the kind of congregation I had. Jane Austen would have recognized my kind of ministry.

## COMMUNITY IN AN ATOMISTIC SOCIETY

It is hard not to feel nostalgic about this today. In general, the institutions of community life have weakened with a sharp decline in "social capital," that is the tangible and intangible benefits of community involvements. There are almost no places left like a church, where a community gathers regularly on the basis of its geographical proximity, and no shared stock of wisdom to turn to during physical or moral trials. Neil McGregor, the former Director of the British Museum, puts it very clearly:

> We are a very unusual society. We are trying to do something that no society has really done. We are trying to live without an agreed narrative of our communal place in the cosmos and in time.[24]

---

24. *Daily Telegraph*, Oct 11, 2016.

Instead, community life has been hollowed out with the emergence of a radical individualism. In the last few decades loneliness has escalated from personal misfortune into a social epidemic. Attendance at public forums, religious groups, civic organizations, has been steadily declining. People go it alone. More people live on their own, more people spend time on the internet in a world of their own, with the social media often dividing people from each other and reinforcing differences. This is even true with spirituality. "I'm a very spiritual person," people say, "but I don't go to church." Sociologist Robert Bellah calls it "Sheilaism," based on a now famous interviewee who said, "I believe in God. I'm not a religious fanatic. I can't remember the last time I went to church. My faith has carried me a long way. It's Sheilaism, just my own little voice."[25]

One of the features of this individualism is that far less people now have contact with churches. Some areas no longer have a functioning church or a resident ministry. In Scotland, for example, the church is currently embarked on a major program of church closures which could close up to a third of its churches, leaving many communities without any visible church presence. In many churches too the days when congregations could claim to be communities where all ages mixed are only a memory. It may have been the case that one of the reasons Dr. Harrison attended church in *Cranford* was the hope of seeing the young lady he is falling in love with at the service. Today this would be a less realistic strategy.

Today many churches have no children's ministries, or youth clubs, and are served by over stretched ministers. Sometimes in my own United Reformed Church there are ludicrous pastorates, with a minister serving a group of small churches too geographically dispersed to be effective. Pastoral care has certainly suffered and, in some cases, virtually collapsed. When my father spent the last months of his life in an old people's home, I was shocked to see people who had been key office holders in their churches rarely visited, even when their former churches were close by. If you have four churches in four different communities, you cannot simply just drop in to see people in the way I took for granted. It is a sign of the times that at a URC Ministries Committee, the convenor could suggest manses should increasingly be near motorway or major road junctions to enable disparate congregations to be served—so much for the minister as at the core of community life.

---

25. See Bellah, *Habits of the Heart*.

But church is still there. The Avebury congregation was never more than a handful in my experience, but that didn't diminish the significance of Auntie Nellie or Bert Jones. Brightlingsea United Church may only have a dozen worshipers, but that doesn't stop them caring for each other, or decorating the church wonderfully for a flower festival to which 150 people come. After and before the service people smile, shake hands, hug even, and later most churches have coffee where members sit and talk. Flowers are still sent out to the sick or those who have anniversaries. When someone dies the community still gathers to support the bereaved. Even when the congregation is tiny, they can use the building as a community asset. Bill Sewell, a retired URC minister, says of the little struggling church of which he is now a member, that at first "I had erroneously concluded they are more totally (theologically) devoid than practically any other congregation I have ever known. I am slowly coming to realise that for the last decade and more, whether they know it or not, they have been exercising a mission/ministry of which I and mine, maybe also you and yours, and certainly many others as well, stand in acute need. Whether or not they are a growing congregation matters not a jot, so long as they stick at it."[26] In Colchester the best place for my granddaughter to go to a parent toddler group is the local parish church and churches still offer an experience of community. I even belong to the Lion Walk Church walking group. Rachel Reeves, currently the shadow chancellor, says "I believe in the teachings of the Bible and charity and Christianity and caring for others. I like the coming together of people at church to celebrate and share together. My kids sing in the church choir."[27]

For all for the difficulties that now face overstretched clergy and ageing congregations churches are mostly still caring communities. Throughout my ministry my experience has been that congregations tried to care for each other, and for me. I remember the choir member in Sutton who was dying of cancer. Near the end she asked me to tell her honestly what was ahead. "I don't know," I told her. "I only know that God's love for us won't cease." "That's what I think too," she said. And I remember the occasion when the church choir came to her sick room to sing for her. Dry eyes are not always possible.

Then there was the time when I was on a fat-free diet and visiting my church secretary; she offered me cake. "Unfortunately, I'm on a diet." "I

---

26. Email to author, Oct 12, 2024.
27. *Times*, Jan 7, 2023.

## "WHAT LIFE HAVE YOU IF YOU HAVE NOT LIFE TOGETHER?"

know," she said, "I've made it with a special fat-free recipe." Later when her marriage broke up, she was distraught, and I tried to offer her what support I could. Years later dying in hospital in Southampton she sent me a message asking if I could visit her, which I did and a few days later came back again to preach at the funeral. What is important about such moments is not that there is anything out of the ordinary about them, but rather the reverse. There is nothing out of the ordinary about them. I am entirely aware that congregations can be uncaring, unwelcoming, and worse. Those who expect much of them will sometimes be disappointed. But not always. Despite the ambivalence of their life, and the ambiguity of their achievements, they offer pathways into an experience of community that can be life-changing. As Langdon Gilkey puts it, the congregation is a "religious entity" which he defines as "a locus for the sacred . . . an embodiment of human relationships . . . a place where God's grace acts and God is present."

The size of my last church, Trinity Sutton, meant I could no longer quite provide the amount of pastoral care that was possible in a smaller congregation, but anyone in hospital could expect to be regularly visited, as could more elderly members of the congregation or those who were new. Everyone was visited at least sometimes with church visitors supplementing the minister's visiting. Along with the 220 members there were around thirty children in worship and over 200 in the active uniformed organizations which were closely involved with the church. There was a café run by the church which included a person known as "listening ear" to whom they could talk if they had problems, a lunch club, a dining club, a manse wine-tasting group, a younger adults group, a youth group and a women's fellowship. At Christmas or Remembrance Sunday the church would be packed with the wider community, and concerts of classical music (often choral involving an augmented church choir) were put on. The church was popular for weddings. It is ethnically diverse. When I was there it had twenty three nationalities, and a Korean congregation until its pastor was deported. It hosts a refugee center, and a congregation of two hundred newly arrived Hong Kong Chinese now worship there on a Sunday afternoon.

Church is about an experience of community in a society where people are increasingly on their own. It cannot be relied upon to get this right. It is remarkably unchoosey in the people it lets in. It normally depends on volunteers to get jobs done and sometimes you have to take whoever you can get. And yet what a precious thing it is to be together and what a blessing this wonderful, exasperating, community is. As Anne Lamott says:

> You've got to love this in a God—consistently assembling the motleyist people to bring into this lonely and frightening world, a commitment to caring and community. It's a centuries-long reality show—Moses the stutterer, Rahab the hooker, David the adulterer, Mary the homeless teenager. Not to mention all the mealy-mouthed disciples. Not to mention a raging insecure narcissist like me.[28]

Church is a life-saving community.

---

28. Lamott, *Plan B*, 22.

# 6

# THE CHURCH AS MORAL COMMUNITY

WHAT MAKES THE CHURCH so significant to the life of society is that it is a moral community. It was Emile Durkheim, the French sociologist generally regarded as one of the founders of modern social science, who grounded this claim in sociological theory. He was no Christian believer, but he saw that religion could hardly be as common as it was in human society if it performed no valuable social function. It was this he set out to analyze. Durkheim defines religion as "beliefs and practices which unite into one single moral community called a church, all those who adhere to them."[1] He believed that religion is about community: it binds people together (social cohesion), promotes behavior consistency (social control), and offers strength for people during life's transitions and tragedies (meaning and purpose). This takes place through various religious rituals, in which collective beliefs are reaffirmed and the individual expresses their solidarity. He had a wonderful phrase for what happens in worship. He called it "collective effervescence," a ritually induced passion or ecstasy that cements social bonds.

Another sociologist, Alan Aldridge sets it out clearly: "Religion promotes social integration by strengthening the bonds between the individual and the society . . . Religion also performs positive functions for the psyche; quite simply it is good for us."[2] As Durkheim says, "The

1. Durkheim, *Elementary Forms of the Religious Life*, 47.
2. Aldridge, *Religion*, 68.

person who has communicated with his god is not merely a man who sees new truths; he is a man who is stronger. He feels within him more force, whether to endure the trials of existence, or to conquer them."[3] This overstresses the positive; religion can be divisive and damaging, but its positive social function is clear. If not, why would people want to belong, or society historically have seen it as so important to its life? Religion cannot be dismissed as simply "a series of misleading fictions";[4] something vital to society and positive for the believer must be involved.

## FIRSTLY, RELIGIOUS COMMUNITIES PROVIDE STORIES AND RITUALS WHICH HELP PEOPLE MAKE SENSE OF THEIR LIVES

Durkheim saw the fundamental beliefs which shaped human life as essentially social phenomena. In his classic study *The Elementary Forms of Religious Life* he wrote that individuals who make up a social group are bound to one another because of their common beliefs. This is one of the most basic functions of religion. European civilization grew up around a common core of Christian belief and institutions. Christian rituals marked the seasons of the year and the cycles of life. In the communal rituals at Easter and Christmas, at ploughing and harvest, with church ales,[5] maying, processions and holy days, the fabric of society was reinforced. Religion provided a common language of the imagination and belief as well as common cultural products such as popular hymns.

    The same was true for social groups within the wider community. Black churches in America were central to the cultural life of the black community, and spirituals and preaching gave them an identity. "Nobody knows de trouble I've seen; nobody knows but Jesus."[6] Through the spirituals they dreamed of change. "I'm so glad the trouble don't last always. By and by, by and by, I'm going to lay down my heavy load."[7]

---

    3. Durkheim, *Elementary Forms of the Religious Life*, 416.

    4. Durkheim, *Elementary Forms of the Religious Life*, 71.

    5. The church ale was a party or festivity in a parish at which ale was the chief drink. It was typically a fundraising occasion for the parish but included music and dancing.

    6. Budmen, *Worship in Song*, 174.

    7. Rieder, "Songs of the Slaves."

> There is a balm in Gilead
> to make the wounded whole;
> There is a balm in Gilead
> to heal the sin-sick soul.[8]

Here the biblical image is being applied to their own lives as slaves and they turn the Bible's question into an affirmation that there is indeed balm in Gilead, a liberation for the oppressed. Arthur C. Jones, writes:

> "Balm in Gilead" is an especially important song in the spirituals tradition, expressing the ability of enslaved Africans to transform sorrow into joy, to make a way where no way seemed possible. That ultimate message of hope and healing . . . is the product of a creative tension between awareness of painful oppressive circumstances and the simultaneous envisioning of a hopeful future."[9]

The hope of the community is shared and expressed through its shared faith.

> I looked over Jordan and what did I see
> Coming for to carry me home
> A band of angels coming after me
> Coming for to carry me home.[10]

Frederick Douglass, an abolitionist former slave, said they brought home to him the dehumanizing character of slavery, "The mere recurrence, even now, afflicts my spirit, and while I am writing these lines, my tears are falling. To those songs I trace my first glimmering conceptions of the dehumanizing character of slavery. I can never get rid of that conception. Those songs still follow me, to deepen my hatred of slavery, and quicken my sympathies for my brethren in bonds."[11] It is no surprise that the spirituals were a major source of images and inspiration for Martin Luther King in the civil rights movement.

This is a dramatic example, but the same process operates in any religious community. When anything tragic occurred, or war threatened, as a minister I naturally turned to Isaac Watts's "O God our Help in Ages

---

8. Presbyterian Church USA, *Glory to God*, No. 792.
9. Jones, *Wade in the Water*, 127.
10. Presbyterian Church USA, *Glory to God*, No. 825
11. Douglass, *My Bondage and My Freedom*.

Past," and when going through a crisis in my own life the words of another of Watts's hymns came to my mind,

> God is the refuge of his saints,
> When storms of sharp distress invade;
> ere we can offer our complaints
> behold him present with his aid![12]

When I have visited the dying, I have usually found the 23rd psalm ("The Lord is my Shepherd, I shall not want)" the most comforting text to read to them, and often as I read, they joined in. Rather similarly in Islam the phrase "Inna lillahi wa inna ilayhi raji'un" ("Surely from Allah we come, to Allah we are going to return)," is a Quranic command used for comfort in times of difficulty. We might compare the way in the United States the hymn "Amazing Grace" is almost always sung at times of crisis. Aretha Franklin sang it at the White House for President Obama in 2014 and she sang it a year later at the service for a member of the Georgia Senate, Clementa Pinckney, when he was killed at a mass shooting at his church. We misunderstand the function of religion if we see it as an alternative science or a historical source. Religion is a system of meaning expressed through metaphor, symbol, music, song, poetry, and art, which offers insights into what it means to be human. The language of faith gives a story about ourselves.

> I once was lost, but now am found,
> Was blind, but now I see.[13]

## SECONDLY, RELIGIOUS FAITH CREATES A COMMUNITY OF LIKE-MINDED PEOPLE WHO SUPPORT EACH OTHER.

George Herbert was a country parson in Wiltshire in the seventeenth century. He describes the task of the pastor as, "Now love is his business and aim. Wherefore he likes well that his parish at good times invite one another to their houses, and he urges them to it. And sometimes, where he knows there has been or is a little difference, he takes one of the parties, and goes with him to the other, and all dine or sup together. There is much

---

12. Congregational Church in England and Wales, *Congregational Praise*, 488.
13. United Reformed Church, *Rejoice and Sing*, 92.

preaching in this friendliness."[14] I can empathize with that. When I first thought of entering the ministry it was preaching which seemed to matter most. I was going to touch people's lives through words. That proved a good deal more difficult than I imagined. But what proved the thing which probably gave me most satisfaction was the pastoral caring that is at the heart of ministry. Being a naturally shy, rather reserved person, this did not come easily to me. When I later completed the Myers-Briggs personality test it classified me as completely unsuited to ministry—probably rightly. The thought of having to interact with people, even worse go to church social events—was deeply alarming. As someone said to me, "whatever are you thinking of going into the ministry if you don't like talking to people?" So I did a little trial to see whether I could do it if I had to. I went to visit an old lady in Wymondham to see how it went. Fortunately, I picked the right old lady. Once I had asked her "how are you," she was off. I went home greatly cheered.

When I got to my first church it was a steep learning curve. I was ordained in Southampton, and I've never forgotten the first person I visited who was dying. He was sheriff of Southampton and due to be mayor the next year. He kept talking about what he was going to do when he took office, but it was obvious when you saw him, he never would. His wife rather pathetically tried to pretend that he was getting better and kept talking about "When you're Mayor Bob." Week by week as I went to visit him, I saw him getting weaker. I walked up the path by the side of the house shrinking inside. I remember on one occasion after seeing him, going to the church and just sitting down and crying. I had said nothing worthwhile. And yet the weeks I could not visit they obviously missed me. I learned a few things which became a guide. Right answers to questions are rarely important. Just being there is. And I learned not to worry. Just be there.

Funerals have been important to me. Looking out of the window of her room at her home at Amherst, Emily Dickinson saw this link between the minister and death.

> There's been a death in the opposite house
> As lately as today.
> I know it by the numb look
> Such houses have always.

---

14. Herbert, *Country Parson*, 451.

> The minister goes stiffly in
> As if the house were his.[15]

In those moments you certainly do have an entrée into homes you've never visited, as well as those where you have been part of the sometimes difficult approach to death. I would often be called in by the family when death was near or had just occurred. It was a huge privilege, and sometimes nurtured links which lasted through the years. The loss of children I always found terribly difficult to deal with. When Ben Jonson's son Benjamin died at age seven, he wrote:

> Farewell, thou child of my right hand, and joy;
> My sinne was too much hope of thee, lov'd boy.[16]

The words "lov'd boy" nearly move me to tears each time I read it.

I think of a lady whose son committed suicide. I visited regularly for quite a while, never with anything very helpful to say, but just to be there and to care. The bond between us stayed strong right through to her death. Sometimes you are actually able to be of some use. A little while ago I met a couple for the first time in twenty years. I had not always got on well with them. He was chairman of the local Conservative party and as he said to me, he was always dealing with politics; he didn't want to hear it when he came to Church. I was not always able to oblige. "Hello Jean," I said, "good to see you again." "Martin," she said, "I want to thank you for the way you took my mother's funeral. It meant a lot." It is a real privilege to be let into people's lives on such occasions. If one text sums up the pastoral ministry it would certainly be, "Rejoice with those who rejoice: weep with those that weep" (Rom 12:15). Now in retirement I miss such sharing hugely.

The church is a community where people care for each other. At least sometimes, at its best, it is. J. D. Vance grew up in the 1980s in the Scots-Irish community in rural Kentucky, in its own way devoutly religious but also poor and frequently emotionally and educationally disadvantaged. The decline in manufacturing industry went alongside broken homes and various forms of addiction. Facing all that, the church offered the support that desperate people needed.

> For alcoholics, it gave them a community of support and a sense
> that they weren't fighting addiction alone. For expectant mothers,
> it offered a free home with job training and parenting classes.

---

15. Dickinson, *Poems*, 185–86.
16. Gardner, *New Oxford Book of English Verse*, 201.

## THE CHURCH AS MORAL COMMUNITY

> When someone needed a job, church friends could either provide one or make introductions. When Dad faced financial troubles, his church banded together and purchased a used car for the family. In the broken world I saw around me ... religion offered tangible assistance to keep the faithful on track.[17]

It would be unwise to expect that degree of support in all churches. And there was a downside. In Vance's case the church also tended to instill a kind of segregation from the outside world. Church communities can be a world to themselves in a dangerous way. But I have certainly seen church members visiting each other, providing places for people to live, supporting others financially, offering help to people facing deportation, providing babysitters, gardening help, going shopping for people, and simply offering love to each other. There is a Russian saying about a husband and a wife who have grown old together, that they are so close that when one cries the other tastes salt. I have seen that in every Church I have ever been part of.

## THIRDLY, RELIGION PROMOTES THE GENERAL GOOD OF THE WIDER COMMUNITY IN ITS CARE FOR OTHERS.

William Temple said, "The Church exists primarily for the sake of those who are still outside it."[18] That may be an exaggeration, but service to others is at the very heart of the gospel. In the Middle Ages churches provided a whole range of administrative and welfare services, the clergy or monasteries were welfare agencies or doctors to the communities as well as religious providers and most hospitals, educational and charitable institutions had their origins in the church. Christian faith has been a major promoter of philanthropy, take for example the Quaker influence exemplified by the Rowntree family, with Joseph Rowntree building New Earswick at York to model better housing for workers, and his son Seebohm Rowntree carrying out a groundbreaking comprehensive survey into the living conditions of the poor in York. Or the Unitarian George Peabody setting up the Peabody Trust which pioneered social housing with such unheard-of luxuries as separate laundry rooms and space for children to play at a time when London had some of the most horrific slums in Europe.

---

17. Vance, *Hillbilly Elegy*, 94.
18. Recalled as a personal dictum in "Letter from the Archbishop of the West Indies" in *Theology* (1956), vol. 59.

## A SERIOUS HOUSE

As a minister I inevitably found myself in small ways in this tradition. In Southampton my church were members of the Community Relations Council. In Swindon my church set up a rent deposit scheme for the homeless and together with our ecumenical partners employed a youth worker to run an open youth club in the old town. In Birkenhead we hosted a Christmas dinner for the isolated and ecumenically helped launch a credit union. In Sutton we hosted an advice center for immigrants and supported the local MHA (originally Methodist Homes for the Aged). In all my churches members knocked on doors raising money for world development in Christian Aid Week. Such concerns are built into the warp and weft of church, done almost automatically since the gospel is rooted in a care for those disadvantaged and the excluded. We might sometimes fail to live up to it, but we knew it was the gospel.

Though the wider community no longer looks to the church at the great transition moments of life in the way it did, funerals, baptisms and weddings are a service offered to the whole community, not simply the committed. It was almost always a joy taking weddings and it was a privilege taking funerals. Some were more meaningful than others. I have known funerals that I think were simply ghastly, when the minister has not met the family beforehand, or even made a virtue of not talking of their life at the service. It is quite difficult when you have never met the family before. But even then, you can spend time with them and listen to what they have to say. Though what do you say when told that the person's favorite leisure activity was phoning in bets for her neighbors, her preferred bet being an accumulator? You can visit again afterwards and again listen. For a short time, you can sometimes come close to them and what you say and do may really matter. Richard Crossman was a Labour Party intellectual and political diarist. He records how, when his wife was dying, "On Saturday evening I was in hospital with the local vicar, a very fine man, with whom I had a furious argument about immortality over the cups of tea the hospital served without cessation." When she died, he asked the vicar to take the service "provided that he knew quite clearly that he was burying an agnostic, and that I was one too." In the end, it worked out well. "Very adventurously, the padre had determined that we should start with 'To Be a Pilgrim' which would have been a fiasco had not Nye (Bevan) led the singing."[19] Personally, I have always tried to avoid furious arguments in hospitals, but this kind of brief but meaningful relationship is a common

---

19. Crossman, *Backbench Diaries*, 122–23

occurrence. Through leprosy hospitals in the Middle Ages, to Christian Aid and food banks today, Christian communities do, at their best, reach out to the needs of the disadvantaged and the victims of injustice.

## FOURTHLY, THE CHURCH OFFERS AN ALTERNATIVE VISION OF A WORLD TRANSFORMED.

Durkheim's analysis of the social functions of religion related to religion in general—if we are being specific for Christianity, I would want to add a fourth. As with most of us my vision of the Christian faith was influenced by the people who personified it when I grew up. At school and university in the 1950s and 60s that meant Martin Luther King, who was marching and preaching for civil rights. I now know he was a more complicated figure than he seemed then, but for me the images of the young man who came victorious out of Montgomery, who triumphed in Birmingham and Selma and offered a dream that was both the American dream and the biblical dream, convinced me that there was no possibility of a non-political gospel. His oratory was amazing.

> If we are wrong—the Supreme Court of this nation is wrong. If we are wrong—God Almighty is wrong. If we are wrong—Jesus of Nazareth was merely a utopian dreamer and never came down to earth. If we are wrong—justice is a lie. . . . And we are determined here in Montgomery—to work and fight until justice runs down like water, and righteousness like a mighty stream.[20]

Years later I was in Washington for the twentieth anniversary of the "I Have a Dream" speech.

The Christian response to human need is not simply acts of kindness but a search for justice; the church is a kingdom shaping movement, committed to changing the old order into something better. The theological origins of such commitment are at the heart of the Judeo-Christian tradition. It most profoundly originates in the prophetic tradition of the Hebrew scriptures. Something quite extraordinary happened in Israel between the sixth and eighth century BC which offered a revolutionary view of God. In human history, religion has generally been about defining the holy, the sacred, and then designing ways to get access to it: obeying rules, performing rituals, sacrificing animals, and enforcing taboos. By contrast the Hebrew prophets

---

20. Oates, *Let the Trumpet Sound*, 71.

began to offer a radically different concept, a God of justice and mercy. "What does the Lord require of you but to do justice, and to love kindness and to walk humbly with your God?" (Mic 6:8).

> Is not this the fast that I choose:
> loose the bonds of injustice,
> undo the thongs of the yoke,
> to let the oppressed go free,
> and to break every yoke?
> Is it not to share your bread with the hungry,
> And bring the homeless poor into your house? (Isa 58:6–7).

The commitment to justice points to a world transformed:

> For I am about to create new heavens
>    and a new earth;
> no more shall the sound of weeping be heard in it,
>    or the cry of distress. (Isa 65)

It is obvious this is not a practical political program but is a vision which has to be translated into practical measures. Throughout the centuries it has led Christians into social action—the list is indicative not comprehensive!

- Francis of Assisi's ministry to the poor and underprivileged, and his care for nature and animals.
- John Ball and the peasant's revolt: "When Adam delved and Eve span, who then was a gentleman."
- Oliver Cromwell insisting no King can prorogue Parliament.
- John Milton's *Areopagitica*.
- Colonel Rainsborough in the Civil War, "the poorest he that is in England has a life to live as the greatest he."
- Wilberforce and the anti-slavery campaign with its image of a chained slave and the words, "Am I not a man and a brother."
- Shaftsbury and factory legislation.
- Elizabeth Fry's work as a prison reformer.
- Sojourner Truth, an abolitionist and women's rights activist, best known for her speech on racial inequalities entitled "Ain't I a Woman?"
- William Booth and the Salvation Army.

## THE CHURCH AS MORAL COMMUNITY

- Benjamin Waugh, a co-founder of the National Society for the Prevention of Cruelty to Children (NSPCC) after working as a congregational minister in the slums of Greenwich.
- Walter Rauschenbusch, whose pastorate in the Second German Baptist Church in Hell's Kitchen in New York led him to being the key figure in the American Social Gospel movement.
- Seebohm Rowntree's work on poverty in York.
- Desmond Tutu and the anti-apartheid struggle.
- Martin Luther King and the civil rights movement.
- Christian Aid.
- Church Action on Poverty.

At the former sheriff of Southampton's funeral, we sang the hymn "These Things Shall Be," which expressed the central vision of his life:

> Nation with nation, land with land,
> Unarmed shall live as comrades free;
> In every heart and brain shall throb
> The pulse of one fraternity.[21]

Christian faith is the dream that things can be better. As Desmond Tutu has put it, Christians shouldn't just be pulling drowning people out of the river. They should be going upstream to find out who's pushing them in.

No one should imagine this is always on every Christian agenda. Some churches react with horror to it. Billy Graham was emphatic that the Vietnam War was none of his business. "I am a New Testament evangelist, not an Old Testament prophet."[22] The Dutch Reformed Church was a major supporter of apartheid; 80 percent of American evangelicals voted for Donald Trump and seem to imagine support for the right to bear arms is a non-negotiable fundamental of the gospel. Even well-meaning churches quite often are keener on things like food banks and soup runs than on asking why poverty exists. But at the heart of the Gospel is a radical impulse. As Tom Holland says,

> That the Son of God, born of a woman, and sentenced to the death of a slave, had perished unrecognised by his judges, was a reflection fit to give pause to even the haughtiest monarch.

---

21. Congregational Church in England and Wales, *Congregational Praise*, 583.
22. Sherry, *Riverside Preachers*, 131.

This awareness could not help but lodge in the consciousness of medieval Christians a visceral and momentous suspicion: that God was closer to the weak than to the mighty, to the poor than to the rich. Any beggar, any criminal, might be Christ. "So the last will be first, and the first last."[23]

## DOES THE CHURCH STILL FUNCTION AS A MORAL COMMUNITY IN A SECULAR SOCIETY?

Today Durkheim's picture of the church as fundamental to the life of the community no longer holds in the old way. He saw this change coming, recognizing that traditional forms of religion were in terminal decline and predicting they were likely to be replaced by new, more scientific ways of understanding the world. To a large extent that has happened. Most people no longer gain a sense of life's meaning from religious faith, nor does it form a significant part of the socialization process for very large sections of the population. Churches today are not central to the life of most communities.

Granted, however, the resources of declining churches are more limited than they were it would be wrong to underestimate the contribution religious communities still make. Even small churches can still be effective community hubs. In its last days before closure Freemantle URC was a very small church indeed. But it hosted a lunch club for homeless and other people on Sundays. Having nowhere much to go, some of the people would hang around the church as early as 9:30 a.m., when morning worship started. To meet the needs of those waiting for lunch, the church invited folk in at 10:30 a.m., after morning worship, for coffee/tea and biscuits. The premises were used by a Brownie Pack, by children's ballet classes, by an Electrical Repair Clinic and a Men's Shed for lonely men (e.g., widowers) to come and chat and have a cup of tea. There was also the dreaded Annual Panto, which involved the many friends of the Freemantle Faithful Few! Very many small churches still impact in this kind of way on their community.

In Colchester, where I live, churches are active in supporting food banks, soup runs, and Beacon House, a day center for the homeless. Considerable sums of money are raised for Christian Aid and other charities. When the pandemic came black majority churches, mosques, and temples showed their ability to reach their own communities where they were trusted more than the government. Clergy still have a place in the community, which

---

23. *Spectator*, Apr 20, 2019.

enables them, if they are willing to do so, to speak out on local issues. When 550 subpostmasters took the Post Office to court in a group litigation, in an attempt to redress the injustices concerning alleged fraud arising from an error-prone computer system, local clergy were sometimes key community figures in supporting them. When Mrs. Jo Hamilton was accused by the post office of taking £36,000 from the village shop she ran in Hampshire, she had to give up her shop and found it difficult to get a new job due to her criminal record. She made ends meet by doing cleaning jobs for people in her village who did not believe she was guilty. On the radio you could hear the gratitude in her voice that the local vicar was one of those who supported her at her sentencing hearing.[24] I have more than once been the only outsider supporting people at immigration tribunals.

Steve Bruce is a sociologist of religion deeply committed to the secularization thesis and not always sympathetic to churches, but he notes the way that they still provide key venues when there is a local disaster. So, for example when in 2011 four men were killed at Gleision colliery in Gilybebyll, the church of St. John the evangelist was open for people "to light candles, write condolences and sit quiet in reflection."[25] When two little girls were murdered in Soham, the local Vicar, the Rev. Tim Albam, was awarded the MBE for the way he comforted the families and spoke for the community. He commented, "I feel greatly privileged but I must stress that I was only doing what priests who are not in the media spotlight do every day of the year."[26] Looking at such examples Bruce comments,

> The clergy of the state churches and the larger Nonconformist denominations form the only professional group of people who are experienced and fluent in public speaking, who are expected to care for their "neighbours," irrespective of their social worth, wealth, charm or power, and who are generally not self-interested.[27]

When I left Swindon the editorial in the local paper was headed, "Goodbye Rev. We'll Miss You."[28] They were not commenting on anything I did in my church but on the opportunities that being a minister give clergy to be involved in the wider community. In an infinitely more significant way when I was in Merseyside and served on MARCEA (Merseyside

24. BBC News, Oct 2, 2020.
25. *Guardian*, Sep 19, 2011.
26. *Daily Telegraph*, Dec 31, 2002.
27. Bruce, *British Gods*, 67.
28. *Swindon Advertiser*, Aug 16, 1999.

Churches Ecumenical Assembly), I saw the way David Sheppard and Derek Warlock were able to help strengthen community life there. When in 1989 the Hillsborough disaster occurred and 96 people were crushed to death and a further 750 injured at the Sheffield Wednesday football ground, Sheppard made three visits to Anfield, and the memorial service at the Anglican Cathedral drew a congregation of 3,000, with 5,000 more outside. Clearly the numbers largely reflected the grief of a city and its fascination with football, but the church was able to be a focus for a community. As Sheppard's chaplain, Stephen Bellamy, put it, "Bishop David didn't have to say anything, but it was so important that he was there, as the city united in grief."[29]

Data collected by the Church of England said its 16,000 churches were running or supporting 35,000 projects before the Covid-19 pandemic, including 8,000 food banks, 4,000 parent-toddler groups, 5,000 lunch clubs or coffee mornings, 2,700 community cafes, 2,400 night shelters and 2,300 breakfast or holiday clubs for children.[30] An independent study organized by the National Churches Trust and carried out by State of Life reported, "There are currently more food banks than McDonald's in the UK—and churches have played a vital role in setting up and running the majority of them."[31] Other church-based projects include drug and alcohol support groups, mental health and counselling services, youth clubs, after-school care and credit unions. Rather bravely they tried to give a financial value to all this, suggesting that the market value of church-based projects is £2.4 billion a year and the non-market value (social and welfare) as at least £10 billion a year, though such things are by definition impossible to price. The independent Theos report into the United Reformed Church claimed that community outreach emerged as the number-one priority of URC churches. Asked "What are your congregation's top two priorities? Where do you direct money, time, and energy?" a remarkable 71 percent of respondents (289/402) chose "community outreach."[32] Sometimes, of course, the reality may not always match the self-image but often it is remarkable. As the Report found, "Wanting to serve the community is part of the DNA of the URC."[33] There is enough truth in this to make the point.

29. Bradstock, *Batting for the Poor*, 245–46.
30. *Guardian*, Oct 18, 2020.
31. *Guardian*, Oct 18, 2020.
32. Mladin, *United Reformed Church*, 15.
33. Mladin, *United Reformed Church*, 15.

## THE CHURCH AS MORAL COMMUNITY

Durkheim hoped that while the decline of religion was part of modernity, new forms of the sacred could be found which were grounded in the deep conditions of modern life and which might come from one's membership of a particular national community or from one's membership in a universal family of humanity. It is certainly true that a variety of social institutions contribute to our shared life together; the family, educational, social, political, and community organizations. In some places the neighborhood itself does so. But the church, with its active communities in every locality and the wide range of its vision and outlook, was in a unique position to create bonds among people. Its decline has weakened our experience of community, leaving us in a more individualistic atomized society. When you turn a church into a block of flats it isn't only the building that is lost. As David Aaronovitch says, "As an atheist declining religion worries me. . . . If I look out of my window, I see an Anglican church and beyond it a Quaker meeting hall. Just below, out of sight, is a small synagogue. At various times people congregate in these buildings. They greet each other, chant, sing and collect for good causes. I simply don't believe life around here would be better if they stopped. In fact, I believe the opposite."[34]

---

34. *Times*, Nov 30, 2022.

# 7

# LOST IN WONDER, LOVE, AND PRAISE

Thomas Troeger tells of being at a performance of Anton Bruckner's First Symphony.

> The standing ovation went on and on. The audience members were stomping their feet, clapping as loudly as they could, and shouting "Bravo, Bravo." . . . As the ovation continued my wife turned to me and asked, "Can we sing the doxology now?" She was serious . . . standing was not enough. Stomping our feet was not enough. Shouting "bravo" was not enough. Applause was not enough. Something more than an ovation had been awaked in her soul and mine.[1]

Music can have that kind effect on us. It can occasion a wonder that moves us to worship. Fred Pratt Green, who like Troeger was both a hymnwriter and a poet, clearly experienced the same.

> How often, making music, we have found
> a new dimension in the world of sound,
> As worship moves us to a more profound
> Alleluia![2]

As ever with worship this is no recent discovery. Michael Spitzer in his *The Musical Human* writes of an age-old link between religion and music, instancing a 40,000 year old bone flute discovered in a cave which was used to play "atoms of music" and the Sumerian priestess Enheduanna

---

1. Troeger, *Wonder Reborn*, 3.
2. United Reformed Church, *Rejoice and Sing*, 414.

(2234–2279 BC), the first recorded name of a composer in the history of the world, "faint echoes" of whose "can be heard in the hymnody of the early Christian Church."[3] Music has the ability to give expression to our deepest feelings about who we are and how we see life and as such is integral to the religious experience.

At the heart of religion is being moved to worship at the mystery, beauty, wonder, and glory of life.

> Holy, holy, holy,
> The Lord God, the Almighty,
> Who was and is and is to come. (Rev 4:8)

Such spontaneous wonder is very different from a church announcing there will be a service of worship on Sunday morning at 10:30 a.m. You cannot program spiritual experience. People will be in church for all sorts of reasons with all kinds of things on their minds. For all, sometimes, and for some perhaps all of the time, the experience may have no deep meaning at all. The experience of worship and the church service may coincide, but you would be unwise to assume it or announce it prematurely.

> They laid this stone trap
> For him, enticing him with candles
> As though he would come like some
> huge moth
> Out of the darkness to beat there.[4]

We meet to confess the mystery, to talk and sing about it and to remind ourselves that it will not ultimately be defined by our words.

## WORSHIP IS THE HEART OF CHURCH LIFE

Although church worship is always shaped by the needs of the congregation, fundamentally it is not about us but our response to God's love. It therefore always properly begins with adoration and thanksgiving. This is not quite how we often see it. Kierkegaard says that people often come to worship in the same frame of mind as if they were attending the theater expecting to enjoy a performance put on by a professional cast: preacher and musicians, etc. But actually, the congregation are the actors and God is the audience.

---

3. Spitzer, *Musical Human*, 180.
4. Thomas, *Collected Poems*, 349.

The analogy is one you can take too far. After all, in the sermon and Scripture reading it is the worshiper who is addressed. But at least it reminds us that worship is God-centered, not a performance to entertain us. We give our praise, express our wonder and love, and make our commitment.

Worship is what unites the church. As the Book of Common Worship of the Presbyterian Church in the USA puts it,

> Worship is at the very heart of the church's life. All that the church is and does is rooted in its worship. The community of faith, gathered in response to God's call, is formed in its worship. Worship is the principal influence that shapes our faith and is the most visible way we express the faith.[5]

Churches do all sorts of things, but this is the primary one without which it is no longer a church. And though it is a response to God, it shapes lives. It reminds us of what matters most, it brings us into an experience of community, it offers us visions by which to live. This, it must be said, is not apparent about many acts of worship. Which of us hasn't come out of church asking if anyone had any idea what the sermon was even supposed to be about! The honest truth is that though I have attended worship nearly all my life, very few of the services stay in my mind. Yes, I can remember the odd outstanding sermon, or occasions when the music has moved me, or when I have not wanted the service to end because I was so carried away by it. But most services slip quickly away, even when I am the person leading it. Often if you asked me what I preached on a week or two before I might have trouble remembering. Occasionally people say, "I'll never forget when you said . . ." and I find myself wondering whether it is simply I have forgotten saying it, or if they have wrongly attributed someone else's wisdom to me.

What worship does is often not particular and immediate in effect; often you cannot put your finger on it. But something important may still be going on. Stories are being learned, values are being shared, horizons broadened; perhaps even long forgotten sermons are still influencing who you are. When I was about ten, rather than going out to Junior Church at Shrub End Congregational Church in Colchester, I started staying in for the adult service. I cannot honestly say I remember any of the Rev. Frank Mead's sermons but that did not mean I was unaffected by them. Years later, with my personal life and faith in some chaos, I was greatly helped by coming across the sermons of Harry Emerson Fosdick in a second-hand

---

5. *Book of Common Worship*, 1.

Oxford bookshop. Years later still Frank Mead, then retired, told me Fosdick had influenced his thinking more than any other preacher. Was it pure coincidence that both of us found the same sermons inspiring, or did the fact that I had heard redactions of them in my childhood make them more credible? People influence us, and ideas and values form in us even when their origin is long forgotten. This is one of the reasons the words of hymns are important and need to be serious—often they lodge in our memories, coming to mind years later.

Worship can become part of the intellectual and spiritual environment which forms us and one of the great influences on our lives. Says William Temple: "to worship is to quicken the conscience by the holiness of God, to feed the mind by the truth of God, to purge the imagination by the beauty of God, to open the heart to the love of God."[6] This applies not only to corporate worship but to personal devotion. But there is an honest realism in Theodore Roosevelt's reminder that "You may worship God anywhere, at any time, but the chances are that you will not do so unless you have first learned to worship Him somewhere in some particular place, at some particular time."[7] So, I am grateful to Shrub End Congregational Church, where I first learned how to worship, whether any particular Sunday was interesting or not.

For many this is becoming more difficult to understand as society becomes more secular. Bill Gates says, "Just in terms of allocation of time resources, religion is not very efficient. There's a lot more I could be doing on a Sunday morning."[8] This has some force from someone who until recently was the world's richest man and has been estimated to earn $4250 a second! But what is an efficient use of time? Does reading poetry, contemplating a sunset, or looking at art qualify? What about reflecting on the meaning of our lives, sharing community, and responding to gracious love? These are certainly not very efficient in terms of maximizing income generation. But is that the only, or even the most important, way to judge the quality of a life? When it comes to worship "not a very efficient use of time" is an inappropriate term, utilitarianism at its worst, which deserves John Stuart Mill's response, "Better to be Socrates dissatisfied than a pig satisfied." There are values unique to humans which are not quantifiable in terms of an efficient use of time.

6. Temple, *Nature, Man and God*.
7. Brooks, *Worship Quest*, 39.
8. *Time*, Jan 13, 1996.

A SERIOUS HOUSE

## THE RHYTHM OF THE CHRISTIAN YEAR

In the Congregationalism of my youth the Christian year was observed in a rather rudimentary way. We had outgrown the absurdity of our Puritan ancestors wanting Christmas Day to be like any other, but beyond Christmas and Easter (and Harvest Festival) we were never very conscious of what Sunday it was. This is another of the areas where my tradition let me down because the rhythm of the Christian year catches some of the rhythm of the seasons and of the Christian life, helping us find meaning and connection to the mystery we call God. The celebrations invite us, through the lens of past events, to look within and around for authentic spiritual encounters in the present, and they point us toward a future beyond the horizons of our sight.

It begins with Advent. My gratitude for Advent has deepened over the years. It has the most wonderful hymns:

> O come, O come, Immanuel, and ransom captive Israel,
> That mourns in lonely exile here, Until the Son of God appear.[9]

Not a very cheerful message and the tune is at least 800 years old, a plainsong melody that feels like a Gregorian chant! But the mix of lament and longing is what makes Advent so powerful. Israel mourning in lonely exile is not a bad image of the human condition with Palestine and modern Israel both in dreadful captivity to violence and vengeance still, and with refugees crowding in tiny boats, to say nothing of the whole planet threatened by global warming. It's good to have a time to sit in the darkness, and ponder that darkness, "until the son of God appear." But Advent is also promise and possibility. There is anticipation in the air, things may and will change. T. S. Eliot put it this way:

> I said to my soul, be still, and wait. . . .
> So the darkness shall be light,
> and the stillness the dancing.[10]

Then Christmas. The fourth Gospel introduces the story of Jesus with a stunning metaphor: "The light shines in the darkness and the darkness has not overcome it." There is wonderful music, poetry, the angels singing on the hillside, and the stories that tell of God's glory found in a child.

---

9. United Reformed Church, *Rejoice and Sing*, 126.
10. Eliot, *Complete Poems*, 180.

> What can I give him, poor as I am,
> if I were a shepherd, I would bring a lamb.[11]

At midnight on Christmas Eve the dark is lit by candles and the promise of hope. "Yea Lord, we greet thee, born this happy morning." What possible substitute could there be as powerful?

But as we all know Christmas does not change the world. It did not then and it does not now. Instead, we find ourselves in the darkest, coldest time of winter. It is the time of post-Christmas ennui.

> Once again
> As in previous years we have seen the actual Vision and failed
> To do more than entertain it as an agreeable
> Possibility, once again we have sent Him away.[12]

But all is not the same. At Epiphany we remember the Magi who travel to Bethlehem. It includes the only hymn I know sung to a star, "Brightest and Best of the Sons of the Morning." They must then travel home, back to their old world and lives, but they are uneasy with the old; they cannot forget what they have seen. Life is not just an explosion of meaningless competing energies. We have seen something better. There are hopes we must hold onto.

As we head deeper into winter there is Candlemas—this one has not really got into Reformed consciousness yet but it is powerful. It comes at the fortieth day after the Nativity at a time when the days are beginning to lengthen and we are poised midway between winter solstice and vernal equinox, the last of winter, the first of spring. The now contends with the not yet. The first spring flowers (snowdrops are sometimes called Candlemas Bells) are a promise, but winter is not yet done with, and it is unwise to be too optimistic too soon. Candlemas keeps us in touch with the natural cycle, is full of the poignancy of hopes that are still beyond us, of dreams that have not yet come true. Candles can flicker and go out. We wait, without knowing quite for what.

The darkness intensifies in Lent when we prepare for Good Friday and the desolation of death. Again, this is not really part of my heritage. On Ash Wednesday, in the year 1522, the Swiss reformer Huldrych Zwingli and twelve friends sat down to eat sausages, in a staged provocation,

---

11. United Reformed Church, *Rejoice and Sing*, 162.
12. Auden, "Well, So That Is That" in Harrison and Stuart-Clark, *Oxford Book of Christmas Poems*, 142.

and it became something of a hallmark of the Reformation for people to declare their ecclesiastical loyalties by publicly refusing to keep the Lenten fast. Preaching in Lent at a URC in Suffolk I was told by a lady that in her Scottish Presbyterian youth she had believed Lent was only for the Catholics and the English! Today the fact that many Nonconformists do not keep Lenten disciplines is more likely due to apathy. The loss is ours. Lent is full of themes that demand profundity and honesty. Themes of temptation, struggle, human weakness, of fall and redemption.

> Of Man's first disobedience, and the fruit,
> Of that forbidden tree whose mortal taste
> Brought death into the world, and all our woe,
> With loss of Eden, till one greater Man
> Restore us, and regain the blissful seat,
> Sing, heavenly Muse. . . .[13]

It's a time to look ourselves, what we are, and what change is called for in us. The changing of the colors in church, the Lenten readings and music, the self-denial, all add to this.

Mothering Sunday offers a break from the austerity of Lent. It's not an official church festival and there are no lectionary texts. In fact, the church officially ignores it—which is not a good idea for the wise preacher because it's why a lot of people are in church that Sunday! In the UK and Ireland, it's been celebrated since the sixteenth century and was traditionally the day when workers were given the day off to visit their mothers and their mother church. Today, Mothering Sunday is a day to celebrate the carers in our lives: birth mothers, adopted mothers, fathers who mother us, and mentors, through them to see God's love. "I was to them like those who lift infants to their cheeks. I bent down to them and fed them" (Hos 11:4).

It is inevitably a poignant day because many people will be remembering mothers who died or how they lost children. In my experience there will often be tears, and the preacher must be very careful what they say. Once I remember a woman who told me how, as a single parent, she had given up her child for adoption and still she felt the pain—a pain that was often ignored in the services she went to. Others may have tried desperately for a baby and never been able to have one, and some are looking forward to the experience. It's a moment when past and present and future can come together. I often see it as the Sunday when spring begins, a feeling accentuated when I was in Swindon by the junior church leaders going to

13. Milton, *Poetical Works*, 212.

pick daffodils for the service from a Wiltshire farm, through a landscape full of old memories. On Mothering Sunday, the seasonal cycle and the church year intersect. Deep human experiences point us to divine love.

> If I were hanged on the highest hill
> Mother o'mine, O mother o'mine
> I know whose love would follow me still
> Mother o'mine, O mother of mine.[14]

The story has to get darker yet. At the end of Lent, we turn to the cross. For two thousand years the cross has been the profoundest Christian symbol, delving into the depths of life's good and evil and inspiring incomparable art, music, and poetry. In the *Isenheim Altarpiece* by Matthias Grunewald, Christ's body shows the marks of the whipping he has received, the crown of thorns has long spikes, his head sags lifelessly, while to his left Mary Magdalene raises her hands in agony while his mother swoons. This is Christ in the midst of desolate and seemingly hopeless suffering. Bach's Passion Chorale immortalizes it:

> O sacred head, sore wounded,
> With grief and shame weighed down.
> O royal head, surrounded
> With thorns, thy only crown.[15]

In one of his stories, Langston Hughes, who grew up in a black church in America, describes a passion service:

> As the preacher describes the pounding of the nails into Jesus' hands and feet. "Don't drive it," a woman screamed. "Don't drive them nails! For Christ's sake. Oh! Don't drive 'em." In song I heard my mother's voice cry:
>
> > Were you there when they crucified my Lord!
> > Were you there when they nailed Him to the tree.
>
> The Reverend Duke Braswell stretched wide his arms against the white canvas of the tent . . .
>
> > Oh, it makes me tremble, tremble!
> > Were you there when they crucified my Lord?[16]

---

14. Kipling, *Selected Poems*, 254.
15. United Reformed Church, *Rejoice and Sing*, 220.
16. Hughes, *Short Stories*, 119.

Most of us will be somewhat more restrained but even this white, middle-class introvert has an emotional response. The passion of Christ is no solution to the problem of life's seemingly meaningless suffering, but it offers the promise that, even in life's darkest moments, sacrificial love can reveal the presence of God.

On Easter Day life is resurgent. The music and the poetry express the triumph.

> Death and darkness get you packing,
> Nothing now to man is lacking.[17]

Powerless love has overcome loveless power and Christ is risen. "Thine be the Glory" to tune of Handel's *Maccabaeus* catches the joy:

> No more we doubt Thee, glorious Prince of life;
> Life is naught without Thee; aid us in our strife;
> Make us more than conquerors, through thy deathless love:
> Bring us safe through Jordan to thy home above.[18]

The full power of all this is only possible for those who have been in the darkness first. But if you have, what powerful understandings of life come out of it, and what poetry and music and art has been inspired by it.

After that we have passed the climax of the Christian year, but there is still Pentecost when we celebrate spiritual presence in our lives, Trinity Sunday (which few look forward to and most preachers find themselves out of their depth), and Ascension when in some churches the pascal candle lit on Easter Day is extinguished, and we recognize that now we stand where things are not so plainly seen. I have to say I don't think most people find this later festival very helpful. Near me at Dedham Parish Church is Constable's best religious painting, *The Ascension*. It has an odd history. It was commissioned by Edward Alston, a brewer from Manningtree and Constable's cousin by marriage, for £200, in order to gain favor with the Archdeacon of Colchester, the Rev. John Jefferson, who was responsible for licensing public houses. When Jefferson not only refused to license Alston's hostelries, but also died in December 1821, Alston reneged on the contract at a great loss to Constable—which may be why when it came to the bottom Constable seems to have lost interest. When I go into Dedham Church, I never find it very satisfactory. It looks as if Constable is having problems picturing it—which may be why his Jesus just looks quite awkward. It's hard

---

17. Vaughan, *Complete Poems*, 216.
18. United Reformed Church, *Rejoice and Sing*, 247.

to be sure whether this is the ascension or the resurrection. He is not the only one to find this all rather problematic. Intellectually I can get my mind round the symbolism but my experience is that very few people relate to it—no preacher is likely to find congregations complaining if they omit it. Today I don't think it really works. Which is to say that some symbolism is time restricted. Certainly, none of my own efforts to preach it have ever had much response!

Then autumn, that poignant season, "when green retreats from sight's still ling'ring gaze, (and) fallen nature driven to her knees. Flames russet, auburn, orange fierce from within."[19] In church this mostly means Harvest Festival which used to be hugely popular but is now very much less so when most people have little contact with agriculture anymore. If the British harvest were to fail completely, the shops would no doubt still be full of produce, brought in from all around the world except that everything would cost more, and our carbon footprint would be even bigger. Harvest Festival nonetheless is an opportunity. It may be we still sing "We Plough the Fields and Scatter" (nonsense though some of it is) but a Harvest service which engages the realities of modern life can serve as a reminder of our dependence upon the earth and its produce and that we live within an interdependent and intricate relationship with the earth, its people, and our environment. Perhaps too the reminder of the passing of time may challenge us to use the time we have. *Carpe diem!*

Then comes Remembrance Sunday, when we consider the horror of war. There was a time when it seemed as if this might be fading away with the increasing distance from the two world wars. In fact, with war in the Gulf, Afghanistan, and with ISIS, it became important to have a Sunday not given to the glorification of war but themes of loss and sacrifice and the reality of war. "My subject is War, and the pity of War."[20] Congregations grew, and it could be hugely moving to hear a trumpeter play the last post or listen to the poems of Wilfred Owen. I quite often used Kipling's poem about the loss of his son in the first war.

> "Have you news of my boy Jack?"
> *Not this tide.*
> "When d'you think that he'll come back?"
> *Not with this wind blowing, and this tide.*[21]

---

19. Guite, "Daily Archives."
20. Owen, *Collected Poems*, 31.
21. Kipling, *Selected Poetry*, 90.

Finally, All Saints, when we look beyond life itself. Our lives are rounded with a sleep but also with the hope of glory. This is almost entirely lost in our culture submerged beneath Halloween. This has its origins in pre-Christian autumn festivals principally designed to mark the beginning of the cold dark months, the need for lanterns and fires and the eating of, principally, root vegetables. Today it's essentially a children's festival with a lot of dressing up in which a lot of sweets and chocolate are consumed and children sometimes play trick or treat. Harmless but meaningless. For myself I still like the idea that as we struggle to live out what faith means the witness of all those who have gone before is there to cheer us on and encourage us. The saints will not allow us to be overwhelmed by the world we live in. They will not allow us to give up. They call out to us saying, "Do not be daunted by the enormity of the world's grief. We've been there too and we're with you now." The saints are the wind at our backs, the sun on our face, the music in our hearts, the sacred community cheering us on, sending us courage and strength and hope for today and tomorrow. The most common hymn for the day is "For All the Saints" to Vaughan Williams's wonderful *Sine Nomine*.

> And when the strife is fierce, the warfare long,
> steals on the ear the distant triumph song,
> and hearts are brave again, and arms are strong.
> Alleluia, Alleluia![22]

A good place to end the church year.

For each season there is music, poetry, story, and myth which deepens it and illuminates our human story. As Larkin puts it the church is a place "In whose blent air all our compulsions meet," where all human desires and drives blend into a vision that speaks to every corner of life and gives purpose and structure to human experience. I find it quite difficult to see all this as an inefficient use of available time.

## THE SACRAMENTS

All through the year if you are a Protestant, there are the two sacraments of the eucharist and baptism. Sacraments are "an outward sign of an inner truth"—symbols of God's love to us in Jesus Christ and a means through which we experience it. They are communal actions which give expression

---

22. United Reformed Church, *Rejoice and Sing*, 658.

to the meaning and significance of the Christian story. The Eucharist (thanksgiving), or the Communion, or the Lord's Supper or the Mass, or the Divine Liturgy—all these terms catch some of the meaning of a sacrament which in nearly all churches is seen as central to worship.

In all honesty the sacraments in Nonconformity have not always been quite as central as in theory they are. In the Congregationalism of my youth communion was sometimes a separate service tacked on a couple of minutes after the main services, giving those who wished time to leave. There was often no chalice, and even if there was, there was quite probably no wine in it. Often across the Church the sacraments were domesticated so as to lose their radical edge. But they are powerful symbols and stories which point beyond themselves to God's gracious love. In the communion the bread and wine are broken and offered to us whoever we are, whatever the condition of our lives. The words of institution link this table with that great table of welcome and hospitality that God is preparing for us one day. "You have prepared a table for us," we say in the words of the 23rd psalm, and at that table are gathered the unlikely, the least possible, the unexpected, and yet the most welcome.

This speaks not only about God but about us. There is a story which I rather like about a Norfolk villager going forward for communion in his parish church, and the only place free at the rail was next to the squire. Anywhere else he would always defer to the squire, quite probably doff his cap, so he instinctively held back. But the squire, about to kneel, paused and beckoned the man forward. "Come, he said, we are all equal here." The implication, not always drawn, is that if we are equal at the table, we do not stop being equal when we leave it. The Eucharist gives us our value in the eyes of God and therefore in human community. Jason Bilbury tells of a woman who was at her father's funeral service and denied communion because she was a lesbian. As if the grief of losing her father wasn't enough, she suddenly had to face a blatant and ugly act of discrimination because of her sexual orientation. She had just sat back down in the pew, totally stunned, when the man next to her pulled out a piece of cinnamon candy from his coat pocket. "This is the body of Christ," he said, holding it out to her, "broken for you."[23]

I have always found it most meaningful when (contrary to normal English Free Church practice) people come and receive the elements kneeling before the table. Personally, I find kneeling more emotionally

---

23. Marin, *Communion Is about Equality*.

powerful than receiving a tray in the pews, and when celebrating I love the personal face-to-face contact. "Broken for you Shirley, broken for you, John, broken for you, Segun." When I was at Trinity Sutton, the congregation was mixed racially and educationally. Male and female, black and white, old and young, university professor, MP, teacher, undocumented immigrant, civil servant, nurse, kneeling equally together to receive the bread and wine equally in need of grace and recipients of God's love.

> As Christ breaks bread and bids us share,
> each proud division ends.
> The love that made us makes us one,
> and strangers now are friends.[24]

Donald Hilton sees the importance of this.

> Above all it gives a vision of sharing. One loaf is divided for all to eat. It is a fair distribution. You can't pay more and get two pieces. You can't put your hand up, plead status or haste, and demand to be served before the others . . . the attitudes which naturally surround the table of the Lord's Supper are a prophetic challenge to those contrary attitudes which control national and international politics.[25]

Baptism services I usually enjoy, certainly I have since I got used to holding children! Recently having lunch in Swindon after taking a service at my old church I was touched when a lady came up to me and said, "You baptized my children twenty five years ago. I've never forgotten how you carried them both round the church, one in each arm!" Parents are nervous, hoping their baby won't do something embarrassing. And congregations usually enjoy them most when they do. They can kick, squeal, just occasionally be sick. Sometimes they wriggle and desperately try to move their heads out of the way. It's a primal moment—how many parents have stood just here doing this—sometimes it was here their parents made their wedding commitments to each other—though this is now rarer since the parents are increasingly often not married but still as proud.

Baptism is not simply a generational rite of passage, a way of saying how much this child matters and how much the love of his parents matters but a powerful celebration of God's love for every human being. John Buchanan tells of a delegation of American Presbyterians visiting the First

---

24. United Reformed Church, *Rejoice and Sing*, 447.
25. Hilton, *Table Talk*, 55.

Presbyterian Church in Havana in Cuba and the American minister being asked to participate, which he did, saying, "Anibal, I baptize you."

> It was a powerful experience for all those present, Cuban and American Christians, of the way baptism overcomes barriers of nationality, history, language, politics, all the barriers that separate the human race.[26]

Then there are weddings, regarded as a sacrament by Catholics and Orthodox, but not by Protestants because they are about our love for each other, not signs of God's love for us. Strictly speaking I agree with this, but there is something sacramental about love; our intimate relationships are central to where we find life's meaning and for many, certainly for me, wedding services are some of the great moments in life. I have taken quite a few of these, sometimes two or even three a Saturday in summer, and I nearly always loved them. They are generational communities, often strangely similar. The family proud, the bride hardly believing she looks so beautiful, the groom with tears in his eyes stumbling over the words, most of the time everyone knowing how important this is. Of course, there is strictly speaking no moral need to get married. Most of the couples I married were already living together and phrases such as "living in sin" are just silly when applied to perfectly respectable couples living together, regardless of their gender. But the service dramatizes the vows, makes explicit and deepens the commitment. These are dramatic moments in a mundane world. What follows will not be a romantic dream, as Louis MacNeice reminds us:

> So, they were married—to be the more together,
> And found they were never again so much together,
> Divided by the morning tea, by the evening paper
> By the children and the tradesman's bills.[27]

But they can be significant prompts towards the kind of relationship which led Anne Bradstreet to say of her husband, "If ever two were one, then surely we."[28] And they are fun. They are an example of how being part of a worshiping community adds color and depth to life.

---

26. Buchanan, *New Church*, 62.

27. MacNeice, "Les Sylphides," in Stallworthy, *Love Poetry*, 302.

28. Bradstreet, "To My Dear and Loving Husband," in Batchelor, *Christian Poetry Collection*, 412.

A SERIOUS HOUSE

## WORSHIP IN A WORLD WHICH IS FORGETTING HOW TO

If all this means something intensely to me, it clearly doesn't for increasing numbers of people. Appreciating it depends on knowing, and locating one's life within, the Christian narrative. It depends on a sense of the transcendence. This is not simply part of the life of great numbers of people. One of the ways you can see the changing mood is in funerals. Taking funerals is one of the most rewarding things ministers are called to do. Normally at a funeral service you know what people's needs are and you can speak to them. The service is within the context of Christian belief, often with stirring music such as Elgar's "Nimrod" or Pachelbel's Canon in D. Hymns might include "The Lord Is My Shepherd," "The Day Thou Gavest Lord Is Ended," or "Thine Be the Glory." The liturgy can be wonderful, perhaps Newman's "Go Forth Upon Your Journey, Christian Soul" or his prayer:

> O Lord, support us all the day long of this troublous life, until the shadows lengthen, and the evening comes, and the busy world is hushed, and the fever of life is over, and our work is done. Then, Lord, in thy mercy, grant us a safe lodging, a holy rest, and peace at the last.[29]

Funerals value and dignify life.

Increasingly this means nothing to many people. How can it when there is no shared context of Christian belief? Hymns are rarely known and sometimes, grimly, there are none. Often one or more family member will speak, leaving the minister as a kind of master of ceremonies. The most popular songs to be played now include "My Way" (Frank Sinatra), "Somewhere Over the Rainbow" (Eva Cassidy), "You'll Never Walk Alone" (Gerry & The Pacemakers), "Always Look on The Bright Side of Life" (Monty Python), "Bring Me Sunshine" (Morecambe and Wise) and "Highway to Hell" (AC/DC). One of my own relatives chose the "Blaze Away" march for his final exit at the crematorium. We are a long way from Cardinal Newman. There is no mistaking the direction this is taking us in. Increasingly there are wholly secular services. This may well be honest to where the families are. But there is no suggestion our lives have any meaning beyond the transitory. There are no angels coming to take anyone home.

29. Duffy, *Heart in Pilgrimage*, 227.

The shape of the new age is different. It doesn't know the Christian vocabulary or story. Instead, the growing affluence of society, and the new ideology of consumer choice, has led to a social fragmentation which has undermined collective identities and community organizations. This is an uncongenial culture for religious institutions. People feel free to pick and choose their faith or cannot see the relevance of churches or worship at all. So congregations have declined, and people are less likely to mark the great transitional moments of life in worship.

There is one style of worship, however, which has proved more suited to contemporary culture because it largely accepts its context and works within it. The great exception to church decline, internationally and in Britain, has been the rise of the charismatic movement. Charismatic communities are very diverse in their theology and ecclesiology, and any attempt to articulate an inclusive set of beliefs and practices is problematic. But central to charismatic worship is a stress on the presence and power of the Holy Spirit, offering an ecstatic spirituality that often combines a passionate devotion to Jesus with the promise that believers will experience either special gifts of the spirit, or gifts of health and wealth or both. It is influential in many growing third world churches, in new charismatic churches in Europe and America, and has strongly influenced the worship of many of the traditional churches. In Britain it is seen both in the growth of local indigenous charismatic churches and of immigrant, mostly black majority Pentecostal churches. So, for example, in 2015–20 Hillsong grew by 41 percent, the Redeemed Christian Church of God by 22 percent, and the Vineyard Churches by 30 percent.[30] Simple generalizations need to be avoided. The white middle-class congregation at Holy Trinity Brompton is not a clone of a West African Apostolic Church or an American television evangelist's ministry. But there are common elements. As Monique Ingallsis says:

> "Pentecostal-charismatic" is used to invoke the constellation of twentieth- and twenty-first- century Christian renewal movements that are related to one another as part of a transnational social network connected by shared beliefs and practices—of which music is, of course, key.[31]

---

30. Brierley, *UK Church Statistics*, table 0.2.
31. Ingalls and Yong, *Spirit of Praise*, 3.

Perhaps it would be fair to say that a commonality is a search for a more personal and immediate relationship with God than appears to be on offer in the historic churches. The worship may include speaking in tongues and healing or exorcism. Often the churches are more open to the wider community than was true with the more traditional Pentecostal churches and offer less restrictive lifestyles—which is why switching from them is common. This process has been described as the "circulation of the saints."

From a sociological perspective one of the most notable features of the new churches is the extent to which presentation and worship is secularized. In a way that traditional worship normally does not, charismatic worship accepts the terms of reference given it by a commodified secular culture. Hillsong, for example, which began in Australia, is now influential worldwide and has been described as a "confluence of sophisticated marketing techniques and popular music."[32] It has produced more than forty albums which have sold more than eleven million copies with over thirty gold or platinum awards. It works by marketing an international brand with the tagline "Welcome Home." Its business model (that is not the wrong phrase) is a globalized product with local franchises like McDonald's or Starbucks or the religious equivalent of Taylor Swift or Beyonce. As Tom Wagner says,

> Hillsong's music "product" is one (if not *the*) main driver of its growth—a globalized offering adopted by Christian churches all over the world. Like McDonald's, Hillsong focuses on the consistency of its product, and achieves it by standardizing production and delivery. . . . Like most modern megachurches, Hillsong is structured and operates like a secular business.[33]

Worship centers often resemble halls or a lecture theatre. The architect of Willow Creek North Shore Church, Adrian Smith, best known for the 2,717-foot Burj Khalifa in Dubai, is explicit that it is purposefully designed to look like a community center instead of a church. "It wants to reach people who are intimidated by going into more traditional staid church buildings."[34]

Worship may include contemporary music, drama, and multimedia presentations all designed to appeal to the interests of the congregation with exciting visuals and upbeat music. What might have been the chancel in a

---

32. Wagner, "Branding, Music, and Religion," 6.
33. Wagner, "Branding, Music, and Religion," 4–6.
34. *Chicago Tribune*, Nov 28, 2016.

traditional church is now often the stage where performers with handheld mics intersperse talk and music very much like a TV program. The model is *Saturday Night Live* rather than traditional Christian worship. Hillsong's very professional worship with arm-swaying audience and electronic music is closer to a pop concert than evensong. No great knowledge of the Christian story is required.

Not all charismatic music is loud but quite a lot is. Repetition is common. Brian Wren tells of a worship service with overhead projector. One of the hymns went something like "Jesus, Jesus, Jesus, Jesus, Jesus, Jesus, Jesus, Jesus." And then at the bottom it said *repeat three times*. In Britain in the 1970s the tone of the music was often triumphalist, full of the promise of victory over foes, "Our God Reigns" or "Shine Jesus Shine." More recently it is more often emotionally warm, sometimes more than a little sexual:

> Father, I want You to hold me
> I want to rest in Your arms today.[35]

Much of this is not likely to be to the taste of those who love traditional worship or poetry or who make intellectual demands on worship and may be tempted to dismiss the music as "Four words, three notes, and two hours." The simple fact however is that this style of music can speak to some the traditional church service cannot. As Dan Blyth, then youth minister at a Hillsong Church, put it, "Young people don't understand hymns, you might as well speak in Spanish."[36] One URC minster, Dan Harris, commented on taking his children to a similar charismatic worship service: "As a family we have been attending the lunchtime service of Kings Church Bolton. The boys aren't familiar with a church service which looks more like a gig/cinema trip."[37] Unsurprisingly they felt more at home at the King's church than in the average URC service. As Martyn Percy puts it, "A movement that stresses personal empowerment, intimacy, and love, yet is 'doctrine-lite' (but still with all the fizz of new wine), innovative and novel, may actually turn out to be a highly popular credo for a third millennium."[38]

The accommodation with culture sometimes goes deeper than simply music, architecture, or church organization. One of the developing trends

---

35. Quoted in Percy, *Power and the Church*, 152.
36. BBC 4, July 21, 2021.
37. Dan Harris, private Facebook post.
38. Percy, *Clergy*, 144.

in charismatic theology is what is called prosperity theology, the belief that Christians should expect financial blessing from God. A "health and wealth gospel" has often been an element in Pentecostalism but from the 1960s on it gained a new prominence with key figures like Oral Roberts. Today prosperity theology has been adopted by influential leaders in the charismatic movement in the United States and has spread throughout the world. Key figures were people like Kenneth Copeland and Kenneth Hagin: "If you drive a mere Chevrolet and not a luxury car you have not understood the gospel."[39] On a visit to America, I was staggered to watch Oral Roberts offering his viewers rolls of cloth which, he claimed, had been saturated in prayer by Korean women and would improve the power of your prayer, and a preacher in a poor area of Philadelphia asking his congregation whether they wanted a big car and a house in the suburbs. It is theology for the capitalist age, a faith perfectly designed for our economic system.

It is not simply that the gospel is conflated with consumer greed—it is the poor who are often taken advantage of and exploited by the preachers. As Philip Jenkins argues, poor citizens of impoverished countries often find the doctrine appealing because of their economic powerlessness and the doctrine's emphasis on miracles.[40] In America there was a really strong black social gospel tradition that supplied leaders and ballast to the heyday years of the civil rights movement including Martin Luther King. Today in the black churches that tradition is in decline as the prosperity gospel has all but erased the social gospel in large sectors of Black Christianity, turning prophetic religion on its head, converting the promise into private spiritual deliverance or worldly wealth. The ironic truth is while liberation theology opted for the poor, the poor opted for Pentecostalism, especially in its prosperity versions.

Prosperity theology is not universal in charismatic churches and would be vigorously repudiated by some. But Kate Bowler of Duke University estimates that around fifty of the largest 260 churches in America explicitly teach Prosperity theology and its influence is almost certainly greater than this. As Paul Gifford recognizes, "Many who explicitly repudiate the 'gospel of prosperity' must nevertheless be considered as preaching success, victory, achievement in the capitalist system."[41] This can be very crass indeed as with Kenneth Copeland: "give $1 for the sake of the Gospel, and $100 belongs

---

39. Gifford, *Plight of Western Religion*, 79.
40. Jenkins, *New Faces of Christianity*, 95.
41. Gifford, *Plight of Western Religion*, 81

to you."[42] It can also be quite shameless. At Hillsong, Pastor Brian Houston, in his wonderfully titled *You Need More Money*, published in 2000, said, "We have to become comfortable with wealth." This is embracing consumer culture with a vengeance. When visiting Ghana, I found Winners Chapel, promising God would provide visas to get generous givers to the UK. A quick check on the internet showed that Winners Chapel International in Colchester was advertising a "Financial Fortune" Banquet and promising that "Financial fortune is my heritage." What is most important about faith is not the cross but the promise of goodies, hopefully for all and certainly for the pastor.

All religious faith has to relate to culture, but this is never without risk. For liberals the risks include being so open to secular culture as to lose any sense of the transcendent and of being absorbed by the cultural status quo. But the fact the charismatic movement does not endorse cultural atheism or rationality does not mean the accommodations it has made are not deeply problematic. Prosperity theology is one example. The uncritical white evangelical and charismatic endorsement of Donald Trump in the US, despite his racism, sexism, misogyny, adultery, overweening greed, disregard for the truth, and fundamental disrespect for other people, is another. Brian Wren offers three real concerns.

1) Pragmatism—whatever draws crowds and gets results must be OK.
2) Reflecting the narcissism of the wider culture—focusing worship on my needs and my feelings, not God.
3) Worship is confused with entertainment.[43]

Marshall McLuhan once declared "the medium is the message," part of the meaning of which is that the way the message is transmitted shapes its content. TV evangelists have to make their products as upbeat and dramatic as possible if they are to compete with *Celebrity Love Island* and maximize their income flow. The music marketing operations must bear in mind what sells. As American singer-songwriter Michael Gungor points out, not a single one of the most popular contemporary English-language Christian hymns or worship songs as recorded by Christian Copyright Licensing International is a lament, compared with 70 percent of the

---

42. Gifford, *Plight of Western Religion*, 79.
43. Wren, *Praying Twice*, 148.

psalms. The urge to be upbeat falsifies the Christian life and often vastly oversimplifies and trivializes the mystery of God. Ian Bradley comments:

> we need to be honest in our worship and in our private conversations and encounters with God, expressing all our perplexity, our frustration and, indeed, our sense of God's absence and lack of action, just as the psalmists did. . . . It does not mean that we are without faith . . . But it does involve us in being honest with ourselves, and with God, and not just indulging in the shallow optimism that is the antithesis of real faith and hope.[44]

If you watch a service from Hillsong it is visually indistinguishable from a pop concert; even the very simplified, often repeated words which give it its Christian content are very similar to secular love songs. There is no doubt that this makes it easier for the culturally unchurched to feel at home, but it can seriously limit the depth and challenge of what is being communicated. When loud emotive music, often devoid of content, is linked with an unquestioning fundamentalism and an utterly unchristian adoption of the values of a consumer society, something very simplistic can emerge. Hillsong, for example, is absolutely up to date in its musical tastes and management models but it is committed to the young earth creationist belief that the world is only six thousand years old, that is, about four thousand years after the first hunter-gatherers arrived in Britain. As Thomas Long puts it, "In the short run, it gets you on your feet clapping your hands, but in the long run it cultivates a monotonic, downsized faith, a faith too naïve and simple to handle complexity, too repetitive to deal with real change."[45]

Charismatic worship offers no solution to the church's dilemma in a commodified age. Religions growing out of this context are likely to be spiritually thin and unsubstantial. In any case it needs to be recognized that the growth of charismatic churches in any given year is always less than the general church decline, that growth seems now to be levelling off, and the leadership, and some of the congregations, aging. The charismatic cavalry is not riding to the rescue.

---

44. *Times*, May 1, 2021.
45. Long, *Beyond the Worship Wars*, 59.

## LOST IN WONDER, LOVE, AND PRAISE

## RECOVERING WORSHIP FOR GOD'S SAKE

Church decline and the crisis in worship are part of the same problem—a post-Christendom culture with a limited view of what is real. Christian faith is based on a series of stories that told us that we lived in a significant universe, and which embody a religious understanding of life transmitted through ritual, preaching, music, literature, and art. Increasingly we have come to doubt the story, to cease the rituals, and in its place embrace a consumerist culture with very limited horizons. As Rowan Williams perceptively notes we live in a "flattened landscape" where we lack the tools or images to enable us to open our eyes to other possibilities.[46] Churches are sometimes complicit in this. As Joseph Sittler argues modern life, modern religion, modern churches, seem to be a conspiracy against awe and mystery. He said, "Our congregational life is so deeply sunk in monodimensional and totally secularized culture as largely to have lost ear, eye, and heart for a word or deed that asserts a totally different possibility."[47]

Churches need the confidence and courage to be different and profoundly countercultural. Worship can offer that alternative, open our eyes, and help us dream other and better dreams. For that it needs to be intellectually stimulating, theologically serious, with a sense of beauty and wonder. It is not there to give us easy answers but to reveal the awe and mystery of God. Seeing a church spire or sharing in worship should make us aware of a different perspective on life. For this we need church buildings which are not afraid of Christian symbolism and which themselves speak of beauty and wonder. There is a wonderful comment by Rev. Septimus Harding in the television adaptation of Trollope's *Barchester Towers*: "If there is no music, there is no mystery. If there is no mystery, there is no God. If there is no mystery, there is no faith."[48] Worship can evoke that mystery and wonder and so enable us, momentarily at least, to touch the transcendent.

All worship is flawed and imperfect. Sometimes when I'm leading worship, I find myself reflecting as Dylan Thomas did when walking out of a dinner party: "Somebody's boring me; I think it's me." But if charismatic worship is often cut off from the past, traditional worship can be in a time warp devoid of creativity and imagination, still singing hymns which were

---

46. Williams, *Lost Icons*, 167.
47. Sittler, *Grace Notes*, 30.
48. "Donald Pleasence: Septimus Harding."

culturally archaic when I was a child. No wonder it really is often boring. Yet it does not have to be culturally static. My own Reformed tradition centers on *Ecclesia reformata, semper reformanda—the church reformed and always to be reformed*. That implies a commitment to self-examination and self-criticism, continual reformation in changing times.

As John Buchanan, whose ministry at 4th Presbyterian Chicago was never dull or static, puts it, "The tradition itself is lively. You don't have to make it relevant. You simply need to be open, imaginative, and responsive to the world and to the Spirit." Your worship will be unacceptably thin if you never use Watts or Wesley, or thrill to Handel or Bach, but there is also Iona, Taizé, or modern hymn writers like Thomas Troeger, Marty Haugen, or Brian Wren. There is no reason why Graham Kendrick should be ignored, or Rutter, or Afro-American spirituals, or folk or jazz. As Buchanan says, "I love the fact that the Fourth Presbyterian Church Morning Choir can do an elegant Vivaldi 'Gloria' and close the service with a Dave Brubeck 'Amen.'"[49] At Trinity Sutton it was always a pleasure to supplement the choir and organ with a trumpeter on Remembrance Sunday and with extra musicians and singers for the Messiah at Easter. At Riverside Church in New York the traditional choir is supplemented by a children's choir, a handbell choir, and a gospel choir.

The traditional is not static, but it is an act of vandalism to replace Handel's Messiah or Samuel Sebastian Wesley with something trite and musically banal. It might be thought creativity is only possible in a large church but in fact all that is required is imagination. In May 2021 I was taking the service at Brightlingsea United Church in Essex with a very small congregation, no singing allowed due to the pandemic, and anyway no organist or pianist. It was not a problem. For music I used a CD of the wonderful choir of Immanuel URC in Swindon with its organist Geoffrey Gleed. That meant not only hymns but Rutter's "Look at the World." Then my wife read Emily's Dickinson's poem "Hope is the thing with feathers," which captures the fragility and persistence of hope.

> "Hope" is the thing with feathers -
> That perches in the soul -
> And sings the tune without the words -
> And never stops - at all.[50]

---

49. Buchanan, Conversation, yale.edu/publications/colloquium-journal/september-2004

50. Dickinson, *Poems*, 116.

Afterwards a lady whose husband had just gone into a home with Alzheimer's came to me and told me how the poem had spoken to her.

We live in a fragmented culture with few certainties and no uniting story. I do not suppose this is likely to change any time soon. But there is a great tradition of worship. It has a long history and deep roots, and is still capable of inspiring us and enriching the wider society. There is a huge tradition of hymns and prayers and theology to draw on. We can be creative, but we must not exchange mystery for easy certainty or allow a flattened commodified culture to determine its own priorities. Instead, our worship must be a response to life's wonder and mystery.

> Articulate with measured sound
> the song that fills all things
> for even atoms dance around
> and solid matter sings.[51]

---

51. Troeger, *Borrowed Light*, 58.

# 8

# GATHERED TO HEAR THE WORD

ONE OF THE THINGS you can't help noticing about churches is that they are places where sermons are preached. Not all traditions value preaching equally, and not all services contain it, but it is prominent in the Roman Catholic, Orthodox, and Protestant traditions. However you look at it, preaching is a strange, one might almost say presumptuous, activity.

> Lord, how can man preach thy eternal word?
> He is a brittle crazy glass;[1]

To stand up week by week before a congregation in the belief that what you are about to say may just contain a word from God is audacious to say the least. "Preaching" said Jitsuo Morikawa, "is God's chosen means of redeeming, transforming, and reshaping human history . . . the hope of the world resides in preaching."[2] Fosdick argued, "The preacher's business is not merely . . . to talk about the available power of God to bring victory over trouble and temptation, but to send people out from their worship on Sunday with victory in their possession."[3] These are huge claims, but at the core of Christian belief is the conviction that ours is a God who communicates with us. "In the beginning was the word, and the Word was God" (John 1:1). This communication takes a variety of forms. God, we may believe, communicates through the natural world, through music and beauty, through the life of a Galilean carpenter, through stories of death and

---

1. Herbert, *English Poems*, 84.
2. Sherry, *Riverside Preachers*, 11.
3. Fosdick, *Living of These Days*, 99.

resurrection, but also in worship through the inadequate words of women and men who wrestle with scripture, with their own doubts and questions and faith, and out of this seek to make the biblical hope come alive in the lives of the people who are gathered to hear the Word. Audacious it certainly is.

When I was growing up preaching seemed hugely important. It was the end of the age of the great preachers. Edwin Sangster at Westminster Central Hall, Donald Soper at the Kingsway Hall, and Leslie Weatherhead at the City Temple held semi-legendary status, people travelled from around the country to hear them preach, and stories were told of queues round the block when they were preaching (though actually by then this was less common).[4] In America, by the time I was born in 1947, Harry Emerson Fosdick's ministry at Riverside had already ended, but it was still vividly remembered, and I read his books avidly, while Martin Luther King was making oratorical magic.

It all gave me an unrealistic view of preaching. This, it seemed to me, was how you touched lives as in no other way. It is hugely embarrassing to recall that my decision to enter the ministry was motivated by the dream of what I might achieve as a preacher. Walking back from a particularly dull sermon in the school chapel at Wymondham College, I said to myself, "Someone needs to do better than that, why not me?" I preached my first sermon at the age of sixteen and dreamt of the day when the queues around the church would be for me. It never happened. I worked incredibly hard at preaching, often spending over twenty hours a week preparing sermons, but I discovered that preaching in general, and my preaching in particular, had severe limitations. In the first few years especially, I often preached over people's heads, like the new minister of whom it was said, "Oh, he answered lots of questions no one ever asked and solved a lot of problems we didn't know we had." Gradually it dawned on me that people understood much less than I imagined of what I was saying, were often listening less intently than I wished, and were not always convinced even if they were listening. Anyway, no queues formed.

> I have spread my dreams under your feet;
> Tread softly because you tread on my dreams.[5]

---

4. Hilton, interview.
5. Yeats, *Selected Poetry*, 35.

Any serious talk about preaching needs to be grounded in reality. It is impossible to assess accurately the effectiveness of the average sermon. What is certainly the case is that preaching has a poor reputation. "Don't preach at me" is a standard rebuke and that sermons are boring is a widely held belief. As the American playwright David Mamet said of his generation, "When we attended synagogue and church, we expected the sermon to be boring. And we were seldom disappointed. Leaving the sacred precincts, our thoughts would turn not to God, but to the waiting roast beef and pudding—just rewards for our supernal patience."[6] There is absolutely nothing new in this. In 1857 Anthony Trollope wrote, "There is perhaps no greater hardship at present inflicted on mankind in civilized and free countries, than the necessity of listening to sermons."[7] One wonders if there was ever a time when this was not the general view?

Of course, there will always have been exceptions, and star quality preachers could no doubt keep a congregation rapt, but it is too much to expect that most preachers will come into this category. Perhaps as Aldous Huxley says, "Preaching is an art, and in this, as in all other arts, the bad performers far outnumber the good."[8] The problem however is more subtle than that. Preaching is about making the biblical word contemporary. It is not a lecture or a lesson; it is an interaction through which the Spirit speaks. By the very nature of the exercise therefore not all sermons will be for everyone. Fosdick understood the limitations of preaching, comparing it to a person at a third-story window letting go a drop of medicine in the hope that in would land in the eye of a sick person in the crowd below. The best you can hope for is that sometimes, some sermons will speak to some people.

Having said which, the great claims for preaching have real potency. Indifferent though many sermons undoubtedly are once a week for twenty minutes, or whatever, people gather to bring the great questions of their lives under scrutiny. When John Donne was dying of cancer, he rose from his sickbed to preach one last sermon before the royal court. He declared,

> Our critical day is not the very day of our death, but the whole course of our life. I thank him that prays for me when the bell tolls,

---

6. *Time*, Jun 19, 2021.
7. Trollope, *Barchester Towers*, 46.
8. Huxley, *The Devils of Loudun*.

but I thank him much more that catechises me, or preaches to me, or instructs me how to live.[9]

And the fact is that sometimes they do get through. Through preaching, at least once in a while, God becomes real to us, as Emily Dickinson puts it, in a way "that scalps your naked soul."[10] In 1933 Fosdick preached one of the great anti-war sermons, "The Unknown Soldier." Dick Sheppard, the vicar of St. Martin in the Fields in London, was so moved he wrote to him, and the Peace Pledge Union was formed. I remember sitting and crying when I first heard William Sloane Coffin's sermon on the death of his son, "Alex's Death." When Mark, my own son, died, his words helped shape my response, and echoes of his preaching recurred in mine. Speaking of the ministers of Riverside Church, where Fosdick and Coffin preached, Paul H. Sherry writes:

> Through the years their preaching has related the Christian Gospel with power to the lives of ordinary people and the struggle of a society in search of its soul. In and through their sermons God has come near to us in our times of need; we have been driven to our knees in repentance for our sin; visions of a world closer to God's intention have danced before our eyes; and our despair has again and again been replaced by a renewed hope.[11]

No one should expect that in every church or every sermon. But no one should discount the possibility that it may. Preaching is a chance, Sunday by Sunday, year by year, to ask how we are to live and what really matters about life. The fact that a sizeable percentage of the community would gather to do this is more remarkable than we realized at the time. It introduced a moral and spiritual center to ordinary life which has not been replaced as churchgoing has lapsed. Providing it is taken seriously, it is a chance to probe regularly and deeply into life's mysteries, wonders and challenges. And even when a particular sermon doesn't work, I occasionally console myself with the thought the time need not be entirely wasted. As a character in one of Wendell Berry's novels says, "I weathered even the worst sermons pretty well. They had the great virtue of causing my mind

---

9. Donne, "Death's Duel," in *Complete Poetry*, 587.
10. Dickinson, *Complete Poems*, 315.
11. Sherry, *Riverside Preachers*, 7.

to wander. Some of the best things I have ever thought of I have thought of during bad sermons."[12]

## PREACHING UNDER A GOD-SHAPED HOLE

Today preaching is unmistakably in crisis. Thomas Troeger has a parable of a church where a mosaic of God the Father has fallen in and services are held "under the God-shaped hole."[13] What has happened is that the once widely shared common framework and language of religion is no longer central to our culture. John Donne has a wonderful line which fits our time, "Tis all in pieces, all coherence gone."[14] This does not make for easy preaching. As the Canadian philosopher Charles Taylor reminds us in his *A Secular Age*, we have gone from a society

> in which it was virtually impossible not to believe in God, to one in which faith, even for the staunchest believer, is one human possibility among others . . . Belief in God is no longer axiomatic. There are alternatives. And this will also likely mean that at least in certain milieux, it may be hard to sustain one's faith.[15]

It is not simply that the preacher is reaching out to those who no longer know the Christian story, or that the credibility of the story is more problematic. It is harder for the preacher themselves to be confident of it. The more people doubt what you believe, the more you may doubt it yourself. Assured truths easily become conceivable possibilities, and combining personal faith with intellectual honesty is increasingly difficult. I feel this myself. A sermon which sounds really quite credible preached to a nearly full church can sound a lot less so preached to mainly empty pews!

As a result, there has been a real loss of confidence in preaching in the church. Judgments here are inevitably subjective, but few ministers give preaching the kind of priority that Weatherhead would have done. Few are as confident in the possibilities of preaching as he was. It's very hard to be so when you see fewer and fewer results for what you do. Depressingly, but unsurprisingly, under the God-shaped hole there has been a relative revival of shallow, anti-intellectual forms of faith which do not attempt

12. Berry, *Jayber Crow*, 162.
13. Troeger, *Preaching*, 11–12.
14. Donne, *Complete Poems*, 270.
15. Taylor, *Secular Age*, 3.

to relate faith to knowledge or understanding. Weatherhead for example made a point of wrestling with the great questions of faith and was always involved in a questioning search for what is true, what we can believe with integrity, not just what does the church teach. In his time there were still enough people who had grown up in the church but were now unsure of what they believed, or outside the church but still interested in Christian belief, to make this a promising strategy. Today such people are far fewer and the intellectual gulf much wider. I doubt if he would fill a church today. Instead, as the church has declined, the intellectual quality of its leadership and preaching has also declined. There is a resurgence of a fundamentalism which is about certainty, not truth, and which sits equally loose to scientific, historical, and biblical scholarship. So, we have a revival of creationism, or an embrace of Christian nationalism or prosperity theology. Explaining his rejection of the idea of evolution, Brian Houston, Senior Pastor at Hillsong Church says, "Much of the debate about the origin of life and the universe is speculation. It comes down to a question of belief."[16] No it doesn't, it comes down to facts, scientific enquiry, and intellectual integrity.

The fundamental principle here is that truth is in order to goodness; in other words that goodness results from following the truth.[17] The two are integrally related; an indifference to the truth is a sign of a lack of moral integrity—witness Boris Johnson or Donald Trump. The church remembers and proclaims the words of its Lord: "and you will know the truth, and the truth will make you free" (John 8:32). As John Wesley said, "It is a fundamental principle with us that to renounce reason is to renounce religion, that reason and religion go hand in hand, and that all irrational religion is false religion."[18] To believe in God is to assert the rationality of life, that there is such a thing as truth and our minds can hope to discover some of it. There is a very funny episode of *The Simpsons* in which the Sunday school teacher is getting all sorts of questions she couldn't answer from her class. Finally, she cries, "Couldn't we have blind faith just for once?" That might be understandable in that context, but it is contrary to the very heart of Christian belief that all truth is of God. "Come now and let us reason together, says the Lord" (Isa 1:18). Questions are not to be ducked

16. *Sydney Morning Herald*, Nov 15, 2005.

17. "We are persuaded," the Presbyterians said long ago, "that there is an inseparable connection between faith and practice, truth and duty. Otherwise, it would be of no consequence either to discover truth or to embrace it." (PCUSA Book of Order, F-1.0304: Historic Principles).

18. Wesley, *Works*, 8.

just because they are difficult, nor uncertainties hidden just because they may disturb. In all honesty not all preaching meets this test. Warns Emily Dickinson:

> Much gestures from the pulpit,
> Strong hallelujahs roll,
> Narcotics cannot still the tooth
> That nibbles at the soul.[19]

On the liberal side of the Church the problem is the opposite. Faith continues to be open-ended, but by seeking to adapt to the wider culture it runs the risk of absorbing the pervading secularism to the point where faith loses all significant content. God becomes at best simply a linguistic device to speak of one's own values, and no vision remains that can inspire anyone who has not grown up within the faith community. To take one example, at the heart of Fosdick's ministry at Riverside was the belief that death had been conquered by Christ. As he put it, "If death ends all, then of all wasters God is the worst."[20] Nothing could be less ambiguous. Any Easter Sunday at Riverside you could be certain that the message would be equally clear. One typical sermon ended:

> This mortal must put on immortality. Let that faith this Easter dignify our lives, ground our characters on unshakeable foundations, devote our service to abiding aims, and keep our hope invincible. Hallelujah! The Lord God Omnipotent Reigneth.[21]

Then the three thousand strong congregation, and the choir, would rise and sing the "Hallelujah Chorus."

> And he shall reign forever and ever
> Forever and ever and ever and ever
> (King of kings and Lord of lords).

There was no question what was being confidently affirmed. Today the surveys suggest about a third of Christians don't believe in life after death, nor do a significant number of theologians. At Riverside, the "Hallelujah Chorus" may still be sung, but the theme is more likely to be how to discover hope in dark times than life after death. In her Riverside sermon in 2023

---

19. Dickinson, *Complete Poems*, 243.
20. Fosdick, *What Is Vital*, 230.
21. Fosdick, *Fit to Live With*, 219.

Adriene Thorne linked the experience of resurrection with where you most love to be in the natural world.

> For me it's water, on a boat, scuba diving, swimming, even in the bath. I touch the holy, I know God in the waterways of the world ... resurrection is the unspeakable force and power of an ocean wave. It's the tear inducing color palate of a sunrise or a sunset ... It's the deep peace you feel when you picture your favorite place in the natural world.[22]

These are experiences which give a sense of life's possibility, but can a resurrection experience really be equated with a beautiful sunset or a satisfying bath? In what sense, if any, do they demonstrate that love is stronger than death? Some take it further.

Gretta Vosper is minister of West Hill United Church in Canada, a popular speaker at progressive conferences, and was endorsed by Jack Spong as his heir. The Easter story, she says,

> is the same story of countless people who have poured their lives out to make their world better, more humane, more peaceful. And while we don't mention the characters, places, or details of the Passion narrative, those who know the story will resonate with the underlying themes found in our two Dream Away services.[23]

There is no suggestion here that this has anything to do with life after death or a resurrection in anything other than the most symbolic way. This is the Christian gospel in a totally secularized form to which the "Hallelujah Chorus" is no longer an obvious response. For Vosper, once the Jesus story has been critically examined, "there is little left for us to get a good hold on."[24] At West Hill Vosper removed the Lord's Prayer replacing it with a non-theistic statement of values such as "I hope that I may always try to understand and comfort other people,"[25] which any reasonably well-meaning person should be able to say. We are a long way from Leslie Weatherhead.

Both these responses are disastrous for the preacher. The first destroys the integrity of preaching and confronts the congregation with beliefs which are not intellectually sustainable. The second avoids those dangers at the

---

22. Thorne, "To Be Continued."
23. Vosper, "Easter."
24. Vosper, *With or Without God*, 238.
25. Vosper, *With or Without God*, 253.

cost of having nothing very serious to say about the fundamental questions of faith. One of the great preachers of our time, John Buchanan, said, "as goes preaching, so goes the Church."[26] That is very much the statement of a mainstream Presbyterian whose life and ministry is rooted in a belief in the Word. But most members of congregations rarely read a theology book and can't be relied upon to go to theological discussion groups or classes. What they do is once a week sit before a preacher. Preaching is where theology can touch everyone. As such it is essential to the life and worship of the church and the proclamation of the word to church and world. In which case, "as goes preaching, so goes the Church" is disturbingly close to the mark.

## THE WONDER OF PREACHING

It is easy to feel daunted by all this. It is also wrong. This is not an easy time to preach. Gail Goodwin in her *Father Melancholy's Daughter* imagines an aged priest complaining to his grown-up daughter: "My ministry has been a stop-gap one. I came along too late you see. The Church I wanted to serve started crumbling a long time ago. Nobody gives a damn about symbols anymore."[27] To which I am tempted to say, "So what?" Occasionally, in my less creditable moments, I think I might have preached to larger congregations and have had a securer place in society in Victorian England than today. But preaching is never a matter of calculating what success you are likely to achieve and going ahead if the odds are in your favor. It is saying that which you have to say, to anyone who will listen, and perhaps some who are not listening! Martyn Lloyd Jones understood this when he said,

> What is preaching? Logic on fire! Eloquent reason! . . . It is theology on fire. Are these contradictions? Of course they are not. . . Preaching is theology coming through a man who is on fire. . . a man who can speak about these things dispassionately has no right whatsoever to be in a pulpit; and should never be allowed to enter one."[28]

---

26. Buchanan, "Rev. Dr. John Buchanan, Lester Randall."
27. *Christian Century*, Feb 20, 2007.
28. Lloyd-Jones, *Preaching and Preachers*, 97.

If anything like that is even remotely true, then when you preach, consequential calculations are out of place. It is easier preaching to two hundred than it is to twenty. It all somehow sounds more credible in a fuller church and the jokes go better. But it is a privilege to do either.

There is a widespread view that in a culture where text, audio, video, and internet combine to produce a world of "audio visually cultured people" preaching's day is over. Words are delivered through iPads or blogs or YouTube, and speech coexists with music and visual images. The fact that a web series like *Critical Role* has 2.2 million followers, to say nothing of a social influencer like Li Jiaqi, the King of Lipstick, who apparently has 5.1 million, is evidence of the potential influence of the internet. Some churches are attempting to utilize this in the case of churches like Hillsong, embracing the new to the exclusion of the traditional. This has left many churches confused, not knowing what to do with their inherited methods of communication.

But just because you listen to online media does not mean that you cannot listen to speech, they are not mutually exclusive simply because they exist in the same virtual space. Rightly done, speech has not lost its power. I have seen people sitting entranced for an hour listening to Bishop Spong or Leslie Griffiths. Barack Obama's oratory was spellbinding, and one of the reasons Tony Blair had an advantage over Keir Starmer was his ability with words. Phillips Brooks once famously described preaching as "truth through personality." It is a meeting, an emphatic sharing, in which congregation and preacher interact with each other. No impersonal media can duplicate that. This has become even clearer during the COVID lockdown when congregations wore masks. It's amazing how this impaired preaching because so much is lost when you can no longer see when the congregation smile or look bored or are visibly moved. It felt like preaching blind. The sermon, at its best, is a combination of reason, emotion, and emphatic personal contact which still has huge potential possibility.

The modern context is different. The pace needs to be quicker, and the preacher needs to employ humor, illustrations, and changes of pace and tone to combat attention loss. You don't have a captive audience but one you must work at relating to; you must establish contact with their lives, so they feel "this is for me." None of this is easy, but it is certainly not impossible. Partly because I still value preaching highly, I am nearly always deeply unimpressed by my own preaching. But my experience is that even with inadequate preachers there can be moments of grace. In my first church I learned something of the limitations of preaching. But I also discovered there are moments when the church goes quiet. The shuffling of feet stops. I remember the first time I noticed this. I can't remember exactly the topic of the sermon. But at some point, I talked about the experience of growing old. How strange it was to look in the mirror and realize you were not the person you once were. "Time you old gypsy man will you not stay, pack up your caravan, just for one day."[29] Suddenly it went deadly quiet. I had touched their lives. People were listening. If you can do that it is real preaching. Perhaps, as George Herbert observed about the inadequacy of his writing,

> Whereas if th'heart be moved,
> Although the verse be somewhat scant,
> God doth supplie the want.[30]

If I take a year at random (2005) I see my sermons at Trinity Sutton included:

Any Man's Death Diminishes Me

Let Justice Roll

Loving Even When You Can't Agree

Life Ahead

Politics: A Christian Vocation

Reckoning With Death

The Blood-Stained Maxi

Safeguarding the Integrity of Creation

Seeing God in Creation

The Anatomy of Forgiveness

To Respond to Human Need

Making Poverty History

Making a New Beginning

The People Who Walk in Darkness

Opening Up the Word of God

---

29. Hodgson, *Poems*, 4.
30. Herbert, *Poems*, 174.

Where is God When Disaster Strikes?

Prince of Peace

Let's assume that not all these sermons were as good as the titles, but it strikes me as remarkable that up and down the country people gather in community to face such questions.

In my case what effect did all my words actually have? In all honesty I cannot assess the effects of nearly sixty years of preaching with any degree of certainty. With some of the people I thought I'd helped the effect didn't seem to last, and some of the arguments I used would no longer convince me. On the other hand, no one was more surprised than I when someone (who I never remember meeting) came up to me at general assembly and told me I was the reason he was in the ministry. Or there was the Christmas letter I had from a lady whose father had just died of cancer. It had been a long painful illness, but his faith had given him strength. His daughter told me how affected he'd been by a sermon of mine on life after death. He had come out of church that Sunday and said, "You know, Mary, there is hope, isn't there?" And that hope had stayed with him to the end. Preaching is an act of faith that somehow God can use our words in ways we cannot know. Every one of us who does this has learned and been humbled by the reality that there is more going on than our words.

In a culture with a God-shaped hole preaching is never going to be easy. The reality of the situation needs to be accepted. As Thomas Troeger says, peaching today has to be about "a willingness to live with the God shaped hole rather than rushing to fill it up with the inadequate projections of our nervous hearts."[31] This is not a time for self-assured theology but for a critical, questioning, and searching faith. We need to take the doubts of the world seriously, recognizing that the traditional shape of the faith is no longer credible even to us in our more self-critical moments. As Herbert Farmer, who was a Presbyterian theologian at Westminster College said, preaching fails when it is too small to be true, too confident to be true, and too easy to be true. Rather we need what Fred Pratt Green, in one of his hymns, called "honesty of preaching."[32] But once that is accepted, preaching can still do its work.

Preaching is where ultimate questions are wrestled with, where doubt and belief, needy world and saving truth, human hunger and divine word

---

31. Troeger, *Preaching*, 18.
32. *Singing the Faith*, No 25.

join together. It is where theology catches fire in human lives. It's a unique, and in its own way rather wonderful thing, part of what it means to call the church "a serious house on serious earth." Any community or church which does not value it is losing something irreplaceable. In his autobiography Harry Emerson Fosdick said, "My silent prayer rose each Sunday before the sermon started, "O God, some person here needs what I am going to say. Help me to reach him."[33] Sometimes this miracle of grace occurs.

---

33. Fosdick, *Living of These Days*, 100.

# 9

# FINDING A MEANING FOR LIFE

Religion is a multi-faceted activity. It may include a system of belief, a way of life, a series of activities and rituals and relationships, but it comes together in a sense of meaning which helps us navigate the difficult business of life. It is certainly not the only place where meaning can be found, but it offers a coherent way of doing so rooted in history and lived out in a community, in the case of the Christian church focusing on the life of Jesus and the stories that were told of him. It gives you a framework of belief about who we are, how we should live, what matters in life, and what life's ultimate concerns are. There is nothing theoretical about this. It's a response to life as it is lived which is rooted in ordinary lives and experience.

What can make faith critically important is that life is inherently difficult, not infrequently almost impossible. Every year some of those once-a-year Christmas letters tell us of some tragedy that tears at the heart, and for which there are no festive words. Many of us are lucky, living as we do in a world where people live longer and healthier lives than ever before. But for much of human history life has often been nasty, brutish, and short, characterized often by poverty, war, slavery, misogyny, disease, and exploitation. Even now when for many life is easier than it has ever been, people still die of cancer, or even worse watch their children die of it, face marital breakups, lose their jobs, face dangers or homelessness or discrimination. If we could know at the beginning what we were going to have to face, we might well be daunted by it.

Anyone who thinks this is exaggerated has not been involved in pastoral ministry for forty years. What am I supposed to say to a mother who tells me her daughter was abused by her brother-in-law, the mother whose son has committed suicide, the gay man who has just received death threats, or the minister in the old people's home who can hardly see or walk, who when I ask him "how long have you been in here?" replied "too long." Life is not easy. Never believe anyone who tells you it is.

The question is, how do humans cope with this? How do we make sense of it, find a way of keeping a positive hope alive, find ways of finding meaning, courage, and inspiration? Faith is one way we do so. James Carroll tells how during the Vietnam War he and a number of others were arrested during an anti-war demonstration in Washington. He was a Roman Catholic priest and had never had an experience like this. In the dark of the cell, he felt lost and afraid. But in the next cell to him was the chaplain of Yale University, Rev. William Sloane Coffin.

> At some point in that night, the man in the next cell began to sing, softly at first. His resolute baritone gradually filled the air as he moved easily into the lyric of what you soon recognized as Handel's Messiah: "Comfort, comfort, ye my people." You recognized the voice as that of William Sloane Coffin. Coffin sang as if he were alone on earth, and the old words rose through the dark as if Isaiah himself had returned to speak for you to God. Others in the cell block soon joined.... "The people that walked in darkness have seen a great light."[1]

That may be an extreme case, but it dramatizes what religious faith can mean in lives, giving a perseverance after goodness, a meaning that gives hope in both life and death. It does not change the difficult reality of life, and ought never to pretend it does, but it offers something potentially vital, a community in which life is shared, a promise that our life has meaning and value, and that goodness and love are worthwhile passions.

Jane Goodall, who is sometimes seen as the world's foremost expert on chimpanzees, tells of a visit to Notre Dame Cathedral in 1974 which changed her life. It was quiet and she found herself looking in awe at the great rose window when the cathedral was filled by the sound of an organ playing the "Toccata and Fugue in D Minor" usually attributed to Bach.

> I had always loved the opening theme; but in the cathedral, filling the entire vastness, it seemed to enter and possess my whole self. It was as though the music itself was alive. That moment, a suddenly captured moment of eternity, was perhaps the closest I have ever

---

1. Coffin, *Credo*, ix-x.

come to experiencing ecstasy, the ecstasy of the mystic. How could I believe it was the chance gyrations of bits of primeval dust that had led up to that moment in time—the cathedral soaring to the sky; the collective inspiration and faith of those who caused it to be built; the advent of Bach himself; the brain, his brain, that translated truth into music; and the mind that could, as mine did then, comprehend the whole inexorable progression of evolution? Since I cannot believe that this was the result of chance, I have to admit anti-chance. And so, I must believe in a guiding power in the universe—in other words, I must believe in God.[2]

Such is the promise of religious faith. As Robert Browning put it,

This world's no blot for us,
Nor blank; it means intensely and means good.[3]

It is not insignificant that this realization for Jane Goodall came in a cathedral. Cathedrals are, as Simon Jenkins says, Europe's "finest works of art."[4] Even now, when church attendance is collapsing, cathedral congregations are holding up. And what unites almost all of them is the beauty they strive for and the awe they inspire. It is said that Pugin was so moved by the beauty of Notre Dame that he fainted the first time he saw it, and Sigmund Freud, a very secular Jew, on his first visit, had "a sensation I never had before." Thereafter he returned to Notre Dame "every free afternoon" to be in its presence. "I have never seen anything so movingly serious."[5] Serious it certainly is. The experiences of awe and beauty are fundamental to religion. In the experience of life's complexity something wonderful breaks through our feelings of sorrow and loss. If only for a moment, we feel a sense of delight, even joy. This is wonderfully symbolized in Michelangelo's "Creation of Adam" in the Sistine Chapel where God reaches out to Adam to bring him into life.

Christian faith gives a sense of a cosmic order held together by God in Christ which offers not only redemption but a model for our own lives. If we are thinking of all the things which church gave, this was the most important. You feel it sometimes when you go into an old church and think that here generations learned the story, baptized their children, buried their dead, and found a meaning for their lives. Think for example what baptism

2. Goodall and Berman, *Reason to Hope*, XIII.
3. Browning, *Poems*, 129.
4. Jenkins, *Cathedrals*, LX.
5. *Guardian*, April 16, 2019.

means—it places a child within a frame of reference in which their lives and who they are matter. This is not some random conjunction of cells; this is a unique human being with an identity, an individuality, a name and a dignity whose life, and what they do with it, is important in the ultimate scheme of things. Before they are born God knows who they are. As Wordsworth puts it,

> Not in utter nakedness,
> But trailing clouds of glory do we come
> From God, who is our home.[6]

This is absolutely not something theoretical. When Mark, Margaret's and my first child, was born he was unable to support his own breathing, and it was clear that once he was taken off life support, he would quickly die. One of the first things I did was to baptize him. It felt vitally important that I did so not because he would be less acceptable to God if not baptized but because it was a way of affirming his value, importance, and dignity. This was not simply a child loved by Margaret and myself but a unique human being whose life mattered and who was loved by God. Later, when we did switch off the life support, he died in my arms. When I next preached, I quoted an African American spiritual.

> Looked over Jordan and what did I see?
> Coming for to carry him home,
> A band of angels coming after him
> Coming for to carry him home.
>
> Swing slow sweet chariot.[7]

The experience of loss and suffering remains, but it is within a context of meaning where the value of life and love is affirmed. That is what religious faith can and does do throughout life. At confirmation we recognize the importance of the commitments we make with our life, at our marriage the value we place on a loving relationship, at funerals the continuing significance of the life. Writing in the *Times* Emma Thompson recalls:

> My brother-in-law's wife died aged 37, leaving three children and a baby. His brave quotation at funeral of Blake's words, "man was made for joy and woe has stayed with me." The Australian priest Richard Leonard writes that "when people come for a hatching,

---

6. Wordsworth, *Poetical Works*, 588.
7. United Methodist Church, *United Methodist Hymnal*, No. 703.

matching, or dispatching, many are open to hearing a hopeful word that speaks to the joy or sadness they bring with them. [By] attending to the dignity, beauty and flow of the sacrament we enable them to ask some of the deeper questions and seek the answers about life's meaning and the grounds for faith."[8]

We are of value, the beloved of God; human life matters; justice is central to life; Christ is the human face of God. It is a story found in Scripture, but also in music, poetry, and art. John Buchanan spells out the profound implications of it.

> Whoever you are, wherever you are on your journey; whatever is happening or not happening in your life—facing surgery, grieving a loss, worried about your job, quietly frustrated and frightened because you can't find a job, bumping along, wondering if you are doing the right thing, wondering who you really are. Hear a word from God, a true word, a life-giving word:
>
> Fear not.... I have called you by name. You are mine.[9]

Something like this has been part of the experience of faith through the ages. Of course it needs to be credible, not simply accepted at face value. But it can, does, and has provided a way of understanding and living life which has given meaning and purpose. And yet does the very fact of life's difficulty, which makes religious faith so powerful, not itself invalidate the promise? The fact is that life is not simply hard, it is not fair.

- 8.8 percent of the world's population are undernourished—this means they have a caloric intake below our minimum energy requirement.
- 663 million people globally are undernourished.
- 22 percent of children younger than five are 'stunted'—they are significantly shorter than the average for their age, as a consequence of poor nutrition or repeated infection.
- 9 percent of the world population—around 697 million people—are severely food insecure.
- One-in-four people globally—1.9 billion—are moderately or severely food insecure.[10]

---

8. *Times*, Apr 10, 2021.
9. Sermon, 4th Presbyterian Church, Chicago, January 10, 2010.
10. Ritchie et al., "Hunger and Undernourishment."

The reality of life is that the innocent suffer and the sheer waste of life is monumental.

There are conclusions to draw from this. One is that there is no *deus ex machina* manipulating events to protect the innocent or frustrate the wicked. Babies are born into destitution or to parents who will abuse them. Trains roll into Auschwitz without any divine impediment. According to an apocryphal but illustrative story in America once there was a minister who wanted to stage an object lesson for the members of his congregation on how they should all live together in peace. So the minister placed a lion and a lamb in a cage just outside the entrance to his Church. And every day there they were together in the cage in peace. And people from miles around came to see this remarkable phenomenon. Finally, the governor of the state, intrigued by this feat, sent a delegation to inquire how the minister pulled off the trick. "Oh, there's no trick at all" said the minister "all you need do is put in a fresh lamb from time to time." There is a brutality about life. Any theology that does not take this seriously is itself not worth taking seriously. At this point religion not infrequently retreats into a kind of make-believe which imagines a world as we might like it, rather than as it is.

A significant number of biblical texts offer what are clearly false hopes and illusory promises.

> The Lord is your keeper
> The Lord is your shade at your right hand.
> The sun shall not strike you by day, nor the moon by night,
> The lord will keep you from all evil (Ps 121:5–7).

But life, as Job and later Jesus discovered, is not like that. In February 1945 German bombs destroyed the headquarters of the Presbyterian Church of England in Tavistock Place in London, killing, among others, the general secretary, the financial secretary, the foreign missions secretary, and the assistant general secretary but missing a nearby brothel. Pain and suffering operate indiscriminately, which is why praying to God to protect those we love from COVID or whatever offers only illusory hope. This does not stop churches succumbing to the temptation of offering it.

"God never wastes pain" is a frequent response, which will be news for those who have watched their children starve to death. Or it is suggested that suffering produces character. There can be an element of truth in this. As Ernest Hemingway said, "The world breaks everyone and afterward many are strong at the broken places."¹¹ But it is perhaps well to remember that Hemingway goes on to add, "But those that will not break it kills. It kills the very good and the very gentle and the very brave impartially." Sometimes there is no positive outcome; pain can destroy as well as strengthen. In her *Testament of Youth* Vera Brittain describes the legacy of war: "That's the worst of sorrow, I decided, it's always a vicious circle. It makes one tense and hard and disagreeable, and this means that one repels and antagonizes people—and that means more isolation and still more sorrow."¹²

Sometimes it is suggested that suffering is the result of human free will. This is to a point true. War, callousness, and sometimes famine, are the result of human choices. But disease, aging, and natural disasters are simply given in life, whatever we do, part of what Hamlet calls, "the heartache and the thousand natural shocks that flesh is heir to."¹³ And in any case this attempted explanation requires a God who chooses to improve the human race by means which even the most inhuman parent might hesitate to use. Which raises the possibility of a God who, to quote William Sloane Coffin, looks rather like a "cosmic sadist . . . an eternal vivisector."¹⁴

All of this calls into question the idea of a loving God. As William Blake says, "Joy and woe are woven fine" into the pattern of our lives, so closely attached they cannot be separated. We would do best not to offer any easy solution to all this. Perhaps, for all I know, human life is not possible any other way. At this point we must all grope our way through the darkness. Often the less we say the better. And yet historically it is clear that most people have found it possible to live with this contradiction. Gothic cathedrals were not built in an age with long life expectancy and, if Africa today is more religious than Europe, it is not because life is easier there. Nor when people give up Christian faith is this, in practice, the predominant cause.¹⁵ Suffering it seems does not in practice negate the inner experience of the divine. Instead, often faith acts as a consolation during suffering and offers a way by which suffering can be lived with and even transformed into something positive.

I can be totally personal here. I have been extremely lucky in life. But none of us escape times of grief. I have felt brokenhearted at the death of a

11. Hemingway, *Farewell to Arms*, 226.
12. Brittain, *Testament of Youth*, 493.
13. Shakespeare, *Complete Works*, Hamlet, Act 3, Scene 1, 63–64.
14. Coffin, *Sermons*, vol. 2, 4.
15. See Francis and Richter, *Gone for Good*, 102.

child, faced a broken marriage after which for a year or two I hardly knew how to keep living, lost a father whose last days were dehumanizing, been in hospital for a month after a road accident, had a period of depression after I retired, and a mix of all the other usual human experiences. I have no easy theology that fits all this together. But this didn't invalidate my faith nor cancel the reality of upholding spiritual presence in life. In the pulpit after my son died, I tried to explain how religious faith could come alive in such moments.

> The morning after Mark was born it was hard to know whether he would live or die, but it seemed clear that if he did live, he would probably be physically and mentally handicapped. I made my way back from the hospital to do some necessary telephoning. As I came up Holm Lane, I found one phrase incessantly coming into my mind. "I know that my redeemer liveth." Praise God I do know that. I know that this world is not a cosmic wasteland created by a blind watchmaker but the work of a loving God. I know that there is meaning and purpose to life. I know that not even death can separate us from his love. I know there is power available to strengthen and support me in whatever life can bring.[16]

It never occurred to me this was in some way the will of a pre-determining deity. It was simply part of the normal painful vulnerability of life. My own belief, for what it is worth, is that we cannot have a finite flesh and blood life in any other way. But what I can say with some certainty is that the sheer intensity of suffering makes us open to new directions in life and can make us ask questions about life's meaning more seriously than we might otherwise do. For a while you live at a depth of experience, with an intensity of emotion, which you never normally have. That's why it's then sometimes you make discoveries which you never would in tranquil times. Which is why that which might call religious faith into question can also deepen it. There is no guarantee this will be the result, but it helps explain why religion's power to give meaning to life can coexist with an open-eyed recognition of the difficult realities of life.

There are concepts of God which life ought to make us question. A God who manipulates and controls life, protecting the righteous and punishing the wicked, is incompatible with the randomness of life. But life is shot through with spiritual presence, with awe and wonder and with experiences of the numinous which point beyond themselves to the

---

16. Sermon, Trinity with Palm Grove Church, Birkenhead, 25th January, 1987.

mystery of our being. This can remain the ground of faith. As Simone Weil put it, "Nothing real can be anything like what I am able to conceive when I pronounce the word (God). But that which I cannot conceive is not an illusion."[17] Religion offers a way of making sense of life, an architecture of meaning in which people find shelter and hope, and a community which embodies it. For good, and sometimes for evil, it has been at the heart of our humanity, who we are and how we live. Go into a great cathedral and you are elevated. Go to Salisbury, Lincoln, Norwich, Chartres, and you feel part of a great story which runs through the ages, a foundational narrative for our humanity. Peter Berger defines religion as "the human enterprise by which a sacred cosmos is established."[18] It creates a social world in which we can place ourselves, gives us stories to tell about who we are, helps us cope with the precariousness of life. Hymns and prayers are full of this promise.

> Dear Name! the rock on which I build,
> My shield and hiding place,
> My never-failing treasury filled
> With boundless stores of grace![19]

Today the sacred canopy has largely gone and with it the theological consensus on which religious authority used to rest. Brian Cox, introducing the BBC program *Universe*, gave the current consensus. "We don't need to invent imaginary gods to explain the universe, we can replace them with the real thing."[20] He described our brief lives in a context of a universe which will end in a bleak nothingness. "We are grains of sand adrift in an infinite and indifferent ocean." For consolation we might care to reflect how "everything we love, everything we value" was created by the stars which have given us this brief moment of meaning which is us. Some would go further and suggest that we ourselves are simply illusions, that human consciousness and decision-making are in reality nothing more than chemical processes. Susan Blackmore is blunt: "You may think that I wrote this piece but in fact it was written by memes competing in the pointless universe."[21] Or as Brian Cox puts it, "Life is just chemistry."[22]

17. Weil, *Gravity and Grace*, 103.
18. Berger, *Social Reality*, 34.
19. United Reformed Church, *Rejoice and Sing*, No. 277.
20. *Universe*, BBC 2, October 27, 2021.
21. Brockman, *What Is Your Dangerous Idea*, 190.
22. *Universe*, BBC 2, October 27, 2021.

This does not mean there are no meanings left in life. Some find meaning in music and drama or art. Some find it in trying to improve human life or in their families or in a passion for progressive politics. Science can give meaning. Indeed, in his *The Grand Design*, Stephen Hawking argues that science can now answer "the ultimate question of life, the universe, and everything."[23] Theology is intellectually discredited; "we claim however that it possible to answer these questions purely within the realm of science, and without invoking any divine beings."[24] The answer is M-theory—that a great number of universes were created out of nothing. Since there is no creator, the meaning of life is what you choose it to be. Quite a few people perhaps no longer ask themselves the traditional questions of meaning and suggest such questions do not arise in postmodern culture.

And yet it is not that simple. More than we often realize Christian ideas remain influential in a secularized form even to those who reject the beliefs. The *Times* columnist Matthew Parris is explicit about this.

> I don't believe in God. But I love the Church, pay my subs to All Saints in Elton, sing hymns and delight in the Testaments Old and New. I say my prayers every night not because anyone is listening, but because I always have. Cathedrals fill me with wonder, graveyards with reverence. The inscription on a gravestone in the nearby village of Youlgreave—to an infant who lived only a few months—"Touch'd the Earth and gone to Glory"—brings tears to my eyes. I subscribe to the Friends of Friendless Churches. And it goes deeper. I love both the story and the person of Jesus, who I'm convinced was a real and wonderful man, albeit under a serious misapprehension about paternity.[25]

There are quite a few people like this in the church and even when faith is decisively rejected some of the heritage may linger. In his *Culture and the Death of God*, Terry Eagleton argues that even when abandoning the faith people often carry through much of its impetus into their new beliefs. The great champion of the new atheism, Richard Dawkins, tells of sitting in Winchester Cathedral, listening to the bells peal. "So much nicer than the aggressive-sounding 'Allahu Akbar,'" he tweeted. "Or is that just my cultural upbringing?" Tom Holland comments, "A preference for church bells over the sound of Muslims praising God does not just emerge by

23. Hawking and Mlodinow, *Grand Design*, 19.
24. Hawking and Mlodinow, *Grand Design*, 216.
25. *Times*, Nov 19, 2021.

magic. Dawkins—agnostic, secularist, and humanist that he is—absolutely has the instincts of someone brought up in a Christian civilisation."[26] John Gray puts it succinctly and memorably: "Secular liberals might pause to reflect that they acquired their deepest values by chance from a religion they despise."[27] Sympathy for the outcast, the idea of human rights, the idea of history as moving to a moral conclusion, are all Christian in origin and may outlast their theological genesis. A post-Christian society bears the imprint of its past.

The decline of faith has not left people in despair or society in collapse. But we have lost the story which gave our lives a wider frame of reference, the cultural and institutional base from which our values came and the religious metaphysic which generated them. M-theory may, or perhaps may not, be part of the explanation of why we exist but does not answer the deep questions of our lives. Human beings, including scientists, are motivated by many things such as truth, love, personal integrity, and humanistic ideals. None of this has any discernible connection with M-theory. Perhaps John Berger is right when he says, "'Never again will a single story be told as though it is the only one."[28] But in all this something is being lost. We are spiritual animals open to the mysterious and the transcendent, we are language-using, question-asking, picture-making creatures, who love, create poetry, art, and music, and understand the meaning of moral obligation, even if we don't always act on it. We are part of a world which has beauty and wonder in it. Famously Kant once said:

> Two things fill the mind with ever-increasing wonder and awe, the more often and the more intensely the mind of thought is drawn to them: the starry heavens above me and the moral law within me.[29]

The question is whether our current state of post-truth anarchy in which right and wrong are the contingent products of history, free will does not exist, and our inner selves an illusion, does justice to this. Peter Berger points us to what he calls "signals of transcendence": signs that force us to consider the possibility that humanity and the world are not accidents of chance, but we reflect something greater than ourselves, to

---

26. *Spectator*, 2019.
27. *New Statesman*, Sep 18, 2018.
28. Berger, G., 129.
29. Kant, *Critique of Practical Reason*, Part 2, conclusion.

universal principles of reality upon which existence itself is ordered.[30] This might be a parent's love for their child, the capacity to play, or to hope in the face of death, the conviction that some things are just wrong and must be condemned, or the capacity to laugh. We might well add our aesthetic experiences in art or music or literature. It's what I feel when going from the noisy London streets into the National Galley to look at Botticelli's "Venus and Mars," in which love overcomes war and which radiates beauty. For Stephen Hawking, "The human race is just a chemical scum on an average-sized planet, orbiting around a very average-sized star, in the outer suburb of one among a hundred billion galaxies."[31] Possibly, but as Emerson reminds us:

> in the mud and scum of things
> There always, always something sings.[32]

How do we speak of the wonder of life?

Let me give one example. One of the spiritual highlights of my life was listening to a performance of Elgar's *Dream of Gerontius* at Winchester Cathedral. It centers on the prayers of a man which act as a prism for our own relation to God. Immediately after he dies, Gerontius is carried by the angel to meet God face to face, and from one piercing glance Gerontius sees the utter goodness and love of God and therefore knows his own unworthiness. There is a kind of blinding flash in the orchestra followed by a somewhat strangulated tenor, singing on a rather high note, the words "Take me away. . ." Finally, it ends with the angelic choir singing triumphantly "Praise to the holiest in the heights, and in the depths be praise." What so moved me when I heard it? I think it was the interaction of a great poem with great music, set in architectural splendor, coming together in beauty and wonder. Such moments take us into another dimension of reality. No account of life is serious which does not take them seriously.

Religion can be as dubious in its outworking as anything else in life and its practitioners as self-serving. But through its stories, music, poetry, and rituals it can help us find a meaning to our lives in a way which affirms life. The Labour politician Ed Balls tells of visiting his mother in a care home in Norwich for the first time in sixteen months because of COVID

---

30. Berger, *Rumour of Angels*, 70.

31. Stephen Hawking, Interview with Ken Campbell on Reality on the Rocks: Beyond Our Ken (1995) http://www.youtube.com/watch?v=S3aadgfoGH8 o

32. Emerson, *Poems*, 396.

restrictions. She had dementia and didn't recognize him. But he was able to sing. "Before we go there's just time for my mum's favourite hymn."[33] Religious images and songs have that sort of power. As a minister I have seen this all the time. When I pray the twenty-third psalm with the dying, they very often join in. Before the moment of death, I would use the Nunc Dimittis, "Lord lettest thou thy servant depart in peace." Such words have power.

We should resist the temptation to suggest that religion has answers to everything or a simple meaning for life. Obviously not. But it keeps open the possibility that there is a meaning adequate for the wonder we experience. This is the great human quest for meaning, which science clarifies, expands, but does not replace. A mother takes a baby in her arms. Science can analyze what is going on up to a point. The heart is racing faster, the hormones are going wild, but something else is happening that no test tube can catch. Something serious is going on which demands a serious explanation. Lose this and life becomes empty and shallow as it often is in our enfeebled culture. Faith may not give total answers, but it suggests there are such answers, its images and stories, music poetry and words, suggest a deep seriousness in life and a journey that goes somewhere. If our culture has lost this, it has enfeebled itself.

> for who would lose,
> Though full of pain . . .
> Those thoughts that wander through eternity.[34]

Life is not just an explosion of meaningless, competing energies; it has purpose, a moral center, and a mystery that turns into wonder. Despite an inhospitable cultural environment, we need to go on telling the story and encouraging churches to be more serious about it. Despite all the moral failings of the churches, and the desperate triviality of some contemporary theologies and worship, the church provides a community of life, service, and worship which embodies a story about ourselves which can still take hold of our imaginations. By reminding us that life is a serious business and has moral purpose it speaks to something fundamental in the human experience.

---

33. *Inside the Care Crisis*, BBC 2, Nov 15, 2021.
34. Milton, *Poetical Works*, 235.

## A SERIOUS HOUSE

One of John Betjeman's most powerful poems is about St. Saviour's Aberdeen Park, the church where both his parents and grandparents had married.

> Great red church of my parents, cruciform crossing they knew—
> Over these same encaustics they and their parents trod
> Bound through a red-brick transept for a once familiar pew
> Where the organ set them singing and the sermon let them nod
> And up the coloured brickwork the same long shadows grew
> As these in the stencilled chancel where I kneel in the presence of God.[35]

If we lose all that this stood for, we lose something profound about our humanity.

---

35. Betjeman, *Collected Poems*, 155.

# 10

# YOU NEVER KNOW WHAT YOU'VE GOT TILL IT'S GONE

NOT LONG AGO AN advert showed an attractive young woman in tight white jeans with high boots, a leather jacket seductively open, leaning against a gleaming Harley Davidson motorcycle. Across the top were two words—"TRUE RELIGION," which it seems is the name of a pair of jeans you can buy at Harvey Nicks or Selfridges. It may be closer to the truth than we like to think in a consumer society where life is flattened out, we are soaked with secularity, and spirituality is ignored or trivialized. "The meaning of life is not being dead," says philosopher Tim Bale[1]—an extreme example of setting the bar too low—though perhaps the American Express advertising slogan "Make all your wishes come true" is in the same league?

Churches offer something very different. In Larkin's poem the visitor feels strange in the church, not at home, not fully understanding. He takes off his cycle clips in "awkward reverence." He goofs around. He goes to the lectern and tries out a few sentences in an overloud voice. "Here endeth the reading." He puts an Irish sixpence in the offering. But then, despite himself, he falls silent.

> though I've no idea
> What this accoutred frowsty barn is worth,
> It pleases me to stand in silence here.[2]

---

1. https://philosophynow.org/issues/59/What_Is_The_Meaning_Of_Life
2. Larkin, *Collected Poems*, 98.

## A SERIOUS HOUSE

He knows despite himself that this is a place where people have come in search of something, great moments in their lives have taken place here, "which, he once heard, was proper to grow wise in."

To me there is something absolutely remarkable, perhaps even wonderful, in the fact that such places were in every locality in the way that supermarkets and fast-food restaurants are in ours. But Larkin hasn't caught their full meaning. Church isn't just an awesome place; it's where you meet an invitation to explore the depths of human experience, the mystery of the divine, and a call to a new and better way of living. Church offers symbols, rituals, and stories, which make all this real, and a spiritual community who share the search with you in word and sacrament.

I have not tried to hide the unavoidable fact that if you actually go to the church's worship you may find it a disappointment. It may be trivial or intellectually dishonest. In too many churches you may find a fundamentalism which is only possible by refusing to think. If you are LGBTQIAA+ you may not be welcomed. Possibly you may find a church so diminished by decline that it is only a pale shadow of what churches were. You may find that the church is surviving by adopting the ideology of consumerism, offering you the absurdity of a Jesus who will make you rich, or as Joshua T. Searle puts it, "Attempting to respond to cultural trends, many churches have ended up mimicking the worst features of consumer culture by packaging Christianity into a marketable bundle of theological propositions that can be distributed and sold to religious consumers."[3] All this is a given. "From the crooked timber of humanity, no straight thing was ever made" (Kant).[4] Churches are morally ambiguous and the words *caveat emptor* (let the buyer beware) really are very relevant here about them. But when you look at churches as dispassionately as you can, there is still a great deal of good. Joni Mitchell's lyrics have become an iconic lament for the loss of the beautiful, valued things in our environment, the displacement of meaningful infrastructure, with what was once beautiful now turned into parking lots.

If churches go the loss will be huge even if better uses than parking lots are found for them. Let me try and summarize the positives about churches which reinforce our humanity, our communities, and our faith journeys.

---

3. Searle, *Theology after Christendom*, chapter two.
4. Oksenberg Rorty and Schmidt, *Kant's Idea for a Universal History*, 15.

## WONDERFUL BUILDINGS WHICH GRACE OUR LANDSCAPE

It was a typical afternoon walk. A few miles outside Colchester, overlooking the Stour Valley, is Mount Bures. We went to see the Norman motte built during the time of the anarchy. Next to it we found the largely twelfth-century Church of John the Baptist. The walls are coursed flint rubble with Roman brick quoins, the nave has three rounded twelfth-century windows. It looks as if today it probably has a fairly small congregation, and there were certainly no other visitors the day we were there. But it is full of history and memory. Unexpectedly a plaque says that Canon Collins, the turbulent priest who was one of the founders both of War on Want and CND, worshiped here for twelve years and, more in character, the novelist Ronald Blythe, who loved it, was once lay reader. It is quiet and lovely and you can pray here. East Anglia is full of churches like this.

> What would you be, you wide East Anglian sky
> Without church towers to recognise you by?[5]

It is buildings like this which give England its visual character. Of course, there are ugly churches and vainglorious ones, but wherever you go it is not difficult to be lost in the quiet of a medieval parish church or swept up in glory in some great rose window or feel the intimacy of a smaller chapel where people have worshiped for generations. Their significance is not simply architectural but as sacred space, a reminder of the transcendent and the beautiful. To redirect some words of Larkin, if we lost them, "Our children will not know it's a different country," but it certainly would be—and an infinitely poorer one.

## 2) COMMUNITIES OF PEOPLE.

I have seen so much simple love and goodness expressed in churches as not to be willing to discount it. The former prime minister, John Major, remembers,

> My father was elderly when I was born and, from the time I was nine years old, mostly bedridden. My mother cared for him, and

---

5. Betjeman, https://www.bbc.co.uk/iplayer/episode/p022ktzy/a-passion-for-churches.

rarely left our home. But the Church came to us in the form of our local Vicar, the kind and gentle J. Franklin Cheyne.[6]

How often something like that has been true. All through my life I have seen church members visiting the sick and the elderly, taking people to appointments, running parents and toddler's clubs, helping out in youth groups, and simply being there for each other. I remember when our son died all the flowers we got and the lady who called and said, "We don't know what to say and we don't know what to do" and then handed us a cake. That said it all. Or when we had a daughter, the church member who made her what was to be a much-loved wooden dog to pull around. Or the couple who offered a house to a displaced Korean pastor and his family and later took Ukrainian refugees into their home. That is church—a place where our human journey is made richer by being lived in community.

Not far from Mount Bures is the small village of Chappel—where there is a small United Reformed Church of a very different kind to any of which I was minister. It was originally built as a store for a local builder before opening in 1901 as a Congregational church. It is very rural. Once I was leading the worship and a lady came in late. "Sorry. One of the cows was giving birth." On another occasion she gave me a gift of eggs. "When it comes to chickens what you get out of them depends on what you put in them." On a Sunday the small building resounds with vigorous singing and powerful organ music. I know the church well enough not to imagine there is never discord among its members, but they know each other well enough that, if there is a problem, they will know about it and be there for each other. A few years ago, the church conducted a survey among its members and friends as to why they came. Almost every reply mentioned "friendliness." Larger churches may have greater varieties of social activity, but the small church offers its own sense of community. At a time when individuals are increasingly removed from the traditional networks of civic engagement—family, friends, community organizations—and there is an emerging social epidemic of rising loneliness, falling trust, and declining participation, this is something to value.

---

6. Major, "Conference Speech."

## 3) A MORAL COMMUNITY

Not only is the church a community—it is a *moral* community. Durkheim saw this is one of the most important social tasks the church fulfils. It shows itself in the values which belong at the heart of its life—and shame it when they are ignored. It shows itself in service to others, commitment to justice and peace, and in the character it develops in people.

When I was at school at Wymondham College, I was allowed to cycle into town to worship at Fairland United Reformed Church. My parents were later both members here, and it is where we go as a family for funerals and christenings. It's a quiet, friendly, and small congregation, and you might think nothing had ever happened here. You would be wrong. In 1918, after the Labour MP for South Norfolk, George Edwards, had lost his seat, his friends held a packed meeting in the Fairland Hall. Representatives of all the parties attended, and it was chaired by the church's minister Edwin Russell. Edwards's story epitomizes the old relation between the farm workers union and nonconformity. He was born in Norfolk in 1850. His family were so poor he ended in a workhouse. At the age of six, Edwards went to work for one shilling a week, scaring crows. Because of the need to work he never went to school and couldn't read or write. When he did get money, he spent it on drink. Then his life changed. He campaigned against rural poverty, becoming the general secretary of the agricultural workers union, MP for South Norfolk, and a JP. His autobiography was called *From Crow-Scaring to Westminster*. What changed him? At twenty-two he went one day into a Primitive Methodist chapel, and he never looked back. "I was led to see I had not been pursuing a right course. The faith I then embraced created within me new ideals on life and, although an illiterate and uneducated youth, I became very thoughtful and most strict in my habits, thinking I had to give up everything I had hitherto indulged in."[7] His wife taught him to read and write, and he became a local preacher and started a new life. In this he was one typical of so many who went into the labor movement. Ralph Miliband's *Parliamentary Socialism* quotes a survey sent to the new Labour MPs in 1906 asking which books they had found most useful. Only two mention books of socialist theory. The main intellectual influences were the Bible and writers ranging from Shakespeare and Milton, to Ruskin, and Dickens.[8] Over 60 percent of Labour MPs at this

---

7. Edwards, *From Crow-Scaring to Westminster*, 30
8. Miliband, *Parliamentary Socialism*, 33.

point were Nonconformist. Not all Christians took this path, which in any case represented only one historical moment in the relationship between faith and life commitment. But it is one example of what in various ways has been consistent in Christian life.

I have seen this all my life. It has been the people who give time to help in soup runs or food banks. The people who commit themselves to community relations organizations or refugee centers. The people who drive people to hospital or help out with uniformed organizations or youth groups, or collect for Christian Aid. The people who help in Oxfam shops or in countless other ways serve the community. Christians have no monopoly on any of this but unmistakably Christian faith has been a consistent motivator in social commitment. One of the largest and most inclusive of studies in this field surveyed more than 2,300 faith communities, encompassing nine religions (and, within this, nine Christian traditions) in northwest England. It identified more than five thousand significant "non-worship" projects involving over forty-five thousand volunteers across the region.

> The projects addressed a wide range of issues and user groups: . . . homelessness, racism, crime, drug and alcohol abuse, health, skills development, art, music, and environmental improvements. Across the survey results it was particularly evident that Faith communities are extensively involved in providing services for older people, children and more deprived neighbourhoods in the region.[9]

The motive here is theological. "Seek the welfare of the city, for in its welfare is your welfare" (Jer 29:7).

## 4) LOST IN WONDER LOVE AND PRAISE

Looking around, Larkin's cyclist sees the hymnbooks and the neat little organ. It is apparent to him that here music is played, hymns sung, sermons preached, prayers said, God glorified—worship takes place. This is the fundamental activity that constitutes church. Through it, at least sometimes, the awe, mystery, and beauty of God intersects with our lives. Evaluating it is difficult, but for about five and a half months the advent of COVID meant I was not able to attend public worship. For me, whatever the value

---

9. Northwest Development Agency, *Faith in England's Northwest*, 4

of country walks or online services, they are not any substitute for being together with others in worship. You preach to these people at this moment in time and you feel their responses. Sometimes they lift you, sometimes you sense they are somewhere else! You hear the music resonating, and you sing together. You pray together, and sometimes yawn together. And after and before service people, smile, shake hands, hug even. Nothing of that is replaceable online, even with the virtual coffee hour! Missing it has given me a new awareness of and appreciation for the essential corporateness of worship.

A secular age will find it very difficult to appreciate this or value its loss. Justin Welby and Sir Ephraim Mirvis compared notes on editors when the religious leaders gave a talk at the JW3 center in north London recently. The archbishop of Canterbury said he was invited to do *Thought for the Day* on Radio 4 one Good Friday, but his decision to talk about the crucifixion met with resistance. "There's a bit too much Jesus in this," he was told by the BBC.[10] Cathedral music may be appreciated or church architecture but worship less so. There is no point spending time regretting this. It is the inevitable consequence of a secular age. But it's important to understand what worship is. Worship is our response to the beauty, wonder, and love of God, a response which can change us and commit us, we believe to a deeper love of others. Once a week we center ourselves on life's highest values and meaning. This is most clearly seen at Easter.

On Easter Sunday the congregation is often somewhat larger than usual. I can understand that. If I only came to church once a year, this is the day I would choose. Very probably the flowers are going to be gorgeous, the music stirring, and there will be a note of excitement in the air. But I think there is more to it than that. People come to church on Easter because they know that what this day is about is the most important, most urgent, most compelling matter in the world. Is there any serious reason, in light of all the violence, suffering, and injustice in the world to believe in goodness and to live with hope and resolve and confidence? The answer is unambiguous. At Easter faith confronts the worst with a broken body on the cross but points to a Christ who breaks the power of death. Good Friday is not the last word. Love is stronger than hate and life is stronger than death. He is risen, He is risen indeed. And we too can experience all this.

> My life is like a frozen thing,
> No bud nor greenness can I see:

10. *Times*, Mar 3, 2023.

Yet rise it shall—the sap of Spring.
O Jesus, rise in me.[11] (Christina Rossetti)

Worship is an experience which re-dedicates life and releases its power, where we get a wider perspective on life and what really matters most about it. Even those who don't share the belief may see the value of having in every community a place where this happens week by week.

## 5) PREACHING

The public place where the life of faith intersects most consistently with the realities of human life is in the sermon. When I was at school, I remember Sydney Myers of Princes Street in Norwich coming to preach at college chapel. I was a questioning, searching sixteen-year-old. Images of God change he said. Think of new images of God if the old ones no longer work. That was sixty years ago, but it's still stayed with me. Preaching matters. I suspect there are still a good many people in our churches who come hoping for a word that will challenge their minds and lift up their spirits. The essential task of a Christian preacher is a simple one—to point people to the Galilean carpenter in whom the reality of God is more visible than anywhere else, to go with them to the foot of the cross where many questions still hang unanswered in the air, but where there is a love that grasps and claims.

## 6) THE POWER OF STORY

The stories we tell ourselves help make us who we are. Most of us will be more moved by the (possibly apocryphal) story of Luther nailing his thirty-nine theses to the church door at Wittenberg than by anything he wrote in them. We experience life narratively and weave our own personal stories into larger ones like human progress or science or religion. Often the stories will stay longer than the arguments, which is presumably why Jesus told stories all the time. What better story could there be than that of Jesus as told in Scripture—preaching, music, song, and stained glass? It contains hugely powerful moral teaching and symbols of God present in human life, in death and resurrection, and does this through a life. We can follow him as he enters Jerusalem rejecting the way of violence, as he storms into

---

11. Rossetti, "A Better Resurrection," in Batchelor, *Christian Poetry Collection*, 177.

the temple confronting injustice, as he struggles with his inner agony, is betrayed, spat upon, ignominiously dies but even on the cross forgives, and is then met again in a garden, in bread and wine and as disciples meet. All that can catch the imagination of anyone. It is a story that overturns all expectations, seeing God supremely in one who was outcast and despised, which sees that love as stronger even than death and has given hope to innumerable individuals for two thousand years.

## 7) A PLACE WHERE MEANING IS FOUND

Finally, Larkin's cyclist feels the seriousness of a place where people have found meaning for their lives.

> A serious house on serious earth it is,
> In whose blent air all our compulsions meet,
> Are recognised and robed as destinies.[12]

That much is clearly true. Churches have been places where people have been aware of the eternal in the presence of time. It offers us a cross, the paradoxical promise that we will find ourselves only if we give ourselves away. Douglas John Hall speaks simply and eloquently: "Salvation for self-absorbed creatures like us means to lose our precious selves in the other. When faith is true, Jesus affirms, we feel ourselves, here and there, now and then—graciously liberated from the burden of self, liberated for the other."[13] Week by week that is what the church is about, expressing our love and commitment to God, reminding ourselves of the story of Jesus, and then finding concrete ways of expressing that love in care of others, bringing justice to the oppressed and bread to the hungry. That is not always popular, but it is the heart of the gospel.

Put all that together and you have something quite remarkable. Of course, if you go into churches sometimes you will find it being lived out and sometimes not. But that there are communities which even fitfully live this out is something to value. My first church in Southampton was the smallest, and in some ways least remarkable, of all the churches I served. I was ordained at Freemantle United Reformed Church in Southampton in 1975 and for ten years ministered to the church, loving its people and seeking to reinvigorate its life. It had around a hundred members, fifteen

---

12. Larkin, *Collected Poems*, 98.
13. Bartlett, *Feasting on the Word*, 24.

in the choir and thirty or so in the junior church. I married my wife Margaret there in 1984. As churches go it was quite unexceptional. The building was post-war redbrick of a dignified simple character but with excellent hall, kitchen, and ancillary rooms which offered options for community use. There was a two manual John Compton pipe organ. The congregation was typical of many URC churches, mostly (but not entirely) middle-aged, a mix of social backgrounds but a number of middle-class people no longer typical of the area. I rather doubt if many people had mystic experiences in worship, but there was serious preaching, not afraid to deal with social issues. This was a living tradition. By 1886 the church meeting was discussing the effects of the Crimes Act in Ireland; the church went on to support passive resistance against the Education Act of 1902, which supported Anglican and Catholic schools from general taxation and during the general strike opened a subscription list for the wives and families of the miners. In my time there were a series of excellent organists, good singing, and the choir, quite a few of whom would never have been in professional choirs, delighted in highlights such as Stainer's Crucifixion at Easter or Hugh Robertson's "All in the April Evening." People knew people and supported each other and reached out into the community to care for old people, offered Guide and Brownie groups, playgrounds for children, a place for alcoholics to meet and supported the Community Relations Council, Amnesty International and the World Development Movement. There were drama and badminton clubs. Sadly, the cricket club which used to play at villages in the New Forest, and for which the church ladies made sandwiches, had lapsed before my time! Over the years a good many lives were shaped by being there with a number of people deeply committed to a liberal social gospel. Weddings were celebrated, children baptized and taught, and lives celebrated at their end—some very significant moments in life. They were very nice to their minister. I do not wish to romanticize this. The lives of the members (and the ministers) were not free of moral ambiguity. After my time the choir broke up after an unseemly row between the minister and the organist. It was a small church that attracted limited numbers. In the long run it was unable to resist growing secularization. It was very ordinary but all the more special for being that. As George Eliot says, "for the growing good of the world is partly dependent on unhistoric acts; and that things are not so ill with you and me as they might have been, is half owing to the number who lived faithfully a hidden life, and rest in unvisited tombs."[14] Freemantle URC is gone now, and the community is poorer for its closing.

The church is a morally ambiguous body. Robert Frost said he had a lover's quarrel with the world, and I have one with the church, but I am clear that its loss would be a diminishment of community, faith, and our humanity. It could do with some cherishing. I would go further than this. Christian churches are not simply channels of culture or reminders that life is more than the values of a consumer society suggest. The church is part of the intention of God. Its ultimate value is only explicable within that context. As a community it was founded by the Jesus whose life centered on his advocacy and inauguration of the kingdom of God. It is by its living out of this commitment to a new order that we judge the church. He certainly founded a community, but in prophetic fashion he centered everything on the kingdom. Unless the whole thrust of New Testament study is wrong, it was the kingdom of God above all that Jesus cared for and in the end died for. Serving this kingdom is what the church is for.

Christianity is about an alternative social vision—an alternative to the violence and suffering and poverty that characterize daily life; it's a vision of kindness, compassion, gentleness, and peace. The task of the church is to keep that vision alive and clear and present in the world. "Set your mind on God's kingdom and his justice before everything else" (Matt 6:33). With this goes a critique of religious organizations that forget this fundamental commitment. "Truly I tell you, just as you did not do it to one of these, you did not do it to me" (Matt 25:45). Jesus here is continuing the prophetic message that to know God is to do justice. "Take away from me the noise of your songs, I will not listen to the melody of your hearts. But let justice roll down like waters, and righteousness like an ever-flowing steam" (Amos 5:21–24). The church is not the purpose of Jesus' ministry. It is a means to an end. The people of God are brought together, only to be sent out; they have an end greater than themselves. Dietrich Bonhoeffer gets this right: "The Church is her true self only when she exists for humanity."[15] After a transformational ministry at 4th Presbyterian in Chicago John Buchanan wrote,

> Studies of growing congregations, at a time when mainline denominations are declining numerically, consistently discover that the one characteristic that growing congregations share is

---

14. Eliot, *Middlemarch*, 896.
15. Bonhoeffer, *Letters and Papers from Prison*, 166.

not theology, ideology, or worship styles, but a sense of mission. Growing congregations are focused on the world outside the walls of their buildings and are intentional about translating the theological affirmations they make inside into acts of compassion, love, and justice outside. When institutional survival absorbs a church's energy and imagination and resources, it simply ceases to be very interesting or compelling. When a congregation lives out its faith in and for the sake of its Lord, it is difficult to ignore.[16]

The church is a place where people find themselves valued by God and one another, learn the story of Jesus, and then, like him, find life by giving themselves away in service to others. A lot of the things that it thinks matter, don't matter at all, but this does.

## THE FUTURE OF THE CHURCH

Today churches are closing, and those that are still open are often only a shadow of what they were. Recently when our first grandchild, Olwen, was born I was asked by her mother what I advised as to her spiritual upbringing. The obvious answer would have been from her earliest days bring her into the church community where she can learn the story of Jesus and absorb Christian values. However, the honest truth is that I preach in around thirty URC and Methodist churches in East Anglia. Not a single one has a functioning junior church of the kind that was an expected part of all the churches I ministered to. I was lost for an answer. It is very hard to see how inter-generational growth is possible for such churches.

There are lots of reasons to be pessimistic about the future of the church. It is very hard to see how the current structures can survive in a meaningful way. All my life people have said they can see the tide turning in favor of the church—and they always have been wrong! My own youthful optimism was also unfounded. I have lived all my life in a secularizing society and a declining church, which often was lacking in the analytic honesty that the times required. Even when it saw what it might do it was usually abysmal at putting the analysis into action! But all that time I have seen the spark of transcendence still alive and moments when grace has been real. I have lived in the conviction that David Jenkins was right when he said, "God is, God is as God is in Jesus, therefore there is hope."[17]

16. Buchanan, *New Church for a New World*, 75–76.
17. Jenkins and Jenkins, *Free to Believe*, 77.

Hope needs to be distinguished very clearly from optimism. There is very little reason to be optimistic about the future of the church in this country. But hope is not the conviction that all can be expected to go well. Hope is what you can still have when everything falls apart and logically you can't see the way forward. Hope is a wild possibility—a frail ark riding on the flood, a dove with an olive leaf, a possibility that a crucified carpenter might ever be heard of again. We maintain this hope in community with others, indeed there is really no other way. Together we listen to the story, gather to hear the word, marvel at the beauty and the music, and are equipped to serve. It can still catch our imagination, even in our own inhospitable cultural environment.

Daunting as all this is, what we are going through has a Christian logic to it. The life of the church depends on a constant process of challenge and renewal. In her *The Great Emergence: How Christianity Is Changing and Why*,[18] Phyllis Tickle observes that every five hundred years the church conducts the equivalent of a rummage sale. "About every five hundred years the empowered structures of institutionalized Christianity, whatever they may be at that time, become an intolerable carapace that must be shattered in order that renewal and growth may occur." Old traditions and structures, forms, and practices, are discarded to make room for the new. After things settle down a new, vital expression emerges—think Protestantism after the upheaval of the sixteenth century Reformation. The older structure, now leaner, is more resilient and newly energized—think Roman Catholicism after the Counter Reformation. This argument needs to be treated with some caution. The five hundred year period can at best only be illustrative, and the reform movements themselves are likely to be flawed and often only partially successful. The Reformation for example was regenerative, but it was also over optimistic in some of its major assumptions and in practice both divisive and destructive. But sometimes the faith has to be broken open in order to find renewal. Not everything of course needs to go. As John Buchanan puts it, "There are some items in the church's attic that we shouldn't sell, some things so valuable, so precious, that they must remain and be part of what is emerging, to remind whatever is about to be born what is good and faithful and helpful about this tradition."[19] But it's this willingness to change which renews the faith. Understanding this is one of the great insights of Reformed theology. *Ecclesia Reformata, Semper*

---

18. Tickle, *Great Emergence*, 19–20.
19. Buchanan, "Always Reforming."

*Reformanda*: The church reformed and always to be reformed. It's what Paul Tillich called the Protestant principle; everything must always be open to reformation.

This process is central to much of what is most valuable in Christian faith and history, not only to the Reformed. It is St. Francis critiquing the worldliness of the medieval church, the Benedictine reforms in monastic life, the visionary theology of Hildegard of Bingen, the Reformation seeking to go back to the church's real purpose, John Wesley reaching out to those untouched by the Church, Schleiermacher arguing belief can never be static, the Oxford Movement's renewed sense of beauty, Harry Emerson Fosdick resisting fundamentalism, the social gospel relating faith to industrial society, Barth and Bonhoeffer challenging a complacent and compliant church in Nazi Germany, Martin Luther King challenging racism and militarism, the challenge of the ecumenical movement, *Ut ūnum sint*— "that they all may be one," John XXIII's *Aggiornamento*, Desmond Tutu confronting apartheid, and the Lesbian and Gay Christian Movement (now OneBodyOneFaith) challenging homophobia and transphobia within the Church. Without change traditions stultify and cannot serve the age of which they are a part.

Today we are living in the midst of a seismic shift that we do not understand but out of which I dare to hope a reinvigorated church may come, though it may be that we cannot yet see what this will be like. In her *Young, Woke and Christian: Words from a Missing Generation*, Victoria Turner lists some of the issues which matter to her generation, such as climate change, racial inclusivity, sexual purity, homelessness, food poverty, sexuality, trans identity, feminism, peace-making, interfaith relations, and disability justice, and argues they are gospel issues. None of these are beyond criticism, and the list is certainly selective. But they show how a tradition can be renewed. There is no going back to the place Christianity had in the world of Christendom. But the tradition can change and grow. When in the sixties I was caught up with enthusiasm for John Robinson's New Reformation I had no idea then how dramatic church decline was going to be or how deep the cultural challenge was. Living through it, it sometimes feels more a nuclear meltdown than a rummage sale. But the fundamental insight was correct. We cannot go on as we were; we have to meet the challenge of our time.

Someone who might help us here is Dietrich Bonhoeffer, whose dramatic life story often obscures his real theological significance. From a socially privileged background, he was only fourteen when he first announced his intention to become a minister. Specializing in academic theology he became a lecturer in the University of Berlin. His life was changed utterly however with the rise of Nazism which led him to become a dissident within the church and to work with the anti-Hitler underground. Arrested, he was sent to Tegel military prison and to Buchenwald concentration camp. This immersed him in the world outside the church. Bonhoeffer saw that Christianity was no longer the dominant force in contemporary society and asked searching questions about what this new reality meant not only for academic theology but for Christian existence in a post-Christian world. In April 1944 in Tegel prison he wrote, "What do a church, a community, a sermon, a liturgy, a Christian life, mean in a religionless world?"[20] His particular circumstances meant he was early to face a question the church still is not clear how to answer. But he gave some practical advice. While in prison he wrote:

> but the day will come—when people will once more be called to speak the word of God in such a way that the world is changed and renewed. It will be in a new language, perhaps quite nonreligious language, but liberating and redeeming like Jesus's language . . . Until then the Christian cause will be a quiet and hidden one, but there will be people who pray and do justice and wait for God's own time.[21]

Like Bonhoeffer, in the end, I can go further than simply saying that the church enriches human life, though this is certainly true. The church is God's and God will preserve it. Frankly we don't know what the future of the church will be, and some will never see it. But the church is a serious house on serious earth, it carries the story of Jesus, it tells the story of who we are, it calls us to give away our lives to others, and to find love as life's central meaning,

> And that much never can be obsolete,
> Since someone will forever be surprising
> A hunger in himself to be more serious,
> And gravitating with it to this ground.[22]

---

20. Bonhoeffer, *Letters and Papers from Prison*, 91–92
21. Bonhoeffer, *Letters and Papers from Prison*, 160.
22. Larkin, *Collected Poems*, 98.

# BIBLIOGRAPHY

Allison, Dale. *Encountering Mystery*. Grand Rapids: Eerdmans, 2022.
Austen, Jane. *Mansfield Park*. Harmondsworth: Penguin, 1966.
Bardwell, W. *Temples, Ancient and Modern*. London: N.p., 1837.
Barth, Karl. *Dogmatics in Outline*. New York: Harper & Row, 1959.
———. *Church Dogmatics, Selections*. Edited by Helmut Gollwitzer. Louisville: John Knox, 1956.
Bartlett, David L., and Barbara Brown Taylor. *Feasting on the Word: Preaching the Revised Common Lectionary*. Year A, Volume 2. Louisville: Westminster John Knox, 2010.
Basden, Paul. *Exploring the Worship Spectrum*. Grand Rapids: Zondervan, 2004.
Batchelor, Mary, ed. *The Lion Christian Poetry Collection*. Oxford: Lion, 1995.
Bellah, Robert. *Habits of the Heart*. Berkeley: University of California, 1985.
Béres, Laura. "A Thin Place: Narratives of Space and Place, Celtic Spirituality and Meaning." *Journal of Religion & Spirituality in Social Work: Social Thought* 31 (2012) 394–413.
Berger, John. *G.: A Novel*. New York: Viking Press, 1972.
Berger, Peter. *A Rumour of Angels*. Harmondsworth: Penguin, 1970.
———. *The Social Reality of Religion*. Harmondsworth: Penguin, 1973.
Berry, Wendell. *Jayber Crow*. Counterpoint: Berkeley, 2001.
Betjeman, John. *John Betjeman's Collected Poems*. Enlarged edition. London: John Murray, 1972.
Binfield, Clyde. *Trinity Church Sutton, Centenary Lecture, 2008*. Sutton: Trinity Church, 2008.
Blaxill, Alec. *History of Lion Walk Congregational Church Colchester, 1642–1937*. Colchester: Benham, 1938.
Bonhoeffer, Dietrich. *Letters and Papers from Prison*. London: Collins, 1959.
Bradstock, Andrew. *David Sheppard: Batting for the Poor*. London: SPCK, 2019.
Brockman, John, ed. *What Is Your Dangerous Idea?* London: Pocket, 2007.
Brown, Andrew, and Linda Woodhead. *That Was the Church That Was*. London: Bloomsbury, 2016.
Browning, Robert. *Poems of Robert Browning*. London: Oxford University Press, 1913.
Brierley, Peter, ed. *UK Church Statistics, No 4: 2021 Edition*. Tonbridge: ADBC, 2020.
Brittain, Vera. *Testament of Youth*. London: Virago, 1978.
Brooks, Steven. *Worship Quest*. Eugene, OR: Wipf and Stock.
Bruce, Steve. *British Gods: Religion in Modern Britain*. Oxford: Oxford University Press, 2020.
———. "Late Secularization and Religion as Alien." *Open Theology* 1 (2014) 13–23.

# BIBLIOGRAPHY

Buchanan, John. M. "Always Reforming." Oct 31, 2010. https://www.fourthchurch.org/sermons/2010/103110.html.

———. *A New Church for a New World*. Louisville: Geneva, 2008.

———. "No Story So Divine." Mar 17, 2002. https://www.fourthchurch.org/sermons/2002/031702.html.

———. "The Rev. Dr. John Buchanan, Lester Randall." Nov 6, 2013. https://www.youtube.com/watch?v=wd8lk_titOM.

———. "Truly Precious." https://jmbpastor.wordpress.com/2020/07/29/truly-precious/.

Buchanan, John M., and John W. W. Sherer. "A Conversation on the Contemporary Church and Traditional Worship." https://ism.yale.edu/sites/default/files/files/A%20Conversation%20on%20the%20Contemporary%20Church%20and%20Traditional%20Worship.pdf.

Budmen, David. *Worship in Song: A Friends Hymnal*. Philadephia: Quaker, 1996.

Camroux, Martin. *Keeping Alive the Rumour of God*. Eugene, OR: Wipf and Stock, 2020.

Chamberlain, T. *The Chancel: An Appeal For Its Proper Use*. London, 1856.

Chaucer, Geoffrey. *The Canterbury Tales*. London: Penguin Classics, 2003.

Chesterton, G.K. *The Ballad of St. Barbara and Other Verses*. London: Cecil Palmer, 1922.

"Church 'Colluded' with Sex Abuse Bishop Peter Ball." BBC. Jun 22, 2017. https://www.bbc.com/news/uk-england-40368573.

Church Hymnary Trust. *Church Hymnary*. 3rd ed. Oxford: Oxford University Press, 1973.

Church of England, "Statistics for Mission, 2021." London: Data Services, 2022. https://www.churchofengland.org/sites/default/files/2023-01/2021-statistics-for-mission.pdf.

Cleaves, Richard. "Hymns and Arias: Whatever Happened to Welsh Hymn Singing?" *Congregational History Society*, Autumn 2023, 139–142.

Coffin, William Sloane. *Collected Sermons: The Riverside Years, vol. 2*. Louisville: Westminster John Knox, 2008.

———. *Credo*. Louisville: Westminster John Knox, 2004.

Congregational Church in England and Wales. *Congregational Praise*. London: Independent Press, 1951.

Congregational Union of England and Wales. *Congregational Yearbook 1953*. London, 1953.

Cornick, David. *Under God's Good Hand*. London: United Reformed Church, 1998.

Cox, Harvey. *The Secular City*. Harmondsworth: Penguin, 1968.

———. *When Jesus Came to Harvard*. Boston: Houghton Mifflin, 2006.

Crossman, Richard. *The Backbench Diaries of Richard Crossman*. London: Hamish Hamilton, 1981.

Cubitt, James. *Church Design for Congregations*. London: Smith & Elder, 1870.

———. *A Popular Handbook of Nonconformist Church Building*. London: James Clark, 1892.

Cunliffe, Barry. *Britain Begins*. Oxford: Oxford University Press, 2013.

Dalí, Salvador. *The Unspeakable Confessions of Salvador Dalí*. New York: William Morrow, 1976.

Davie, Grace. *Europe: The Exceptional Case*. London: Darton, Longman and Todd, 2002.

Davies, H. *Worship and Theology in England: Vol 4, From Newman to Martineau*. Grand Rapids: Eerdmans, 1962.

Davis, Ellen. "Wise and Holy Work." *Faith & Form* 38.3 (2005) 6.

Dawkins, Richard. "Atheists for Jesus." *Free Enquiry* (Dec 2005-Jan 2005).

# BIBLIOGRAPHY

Dickinson, Emily. *The Complete Poems*. London: Faber and Faber, 1975.

Dillard, Annie. "The Gospel according to St Luke." In *Incarnation: Contemporary Writers on the New Testament*, edited by Alfred Corn. New York: Viking, 1990.

Dodd, C. H. *The Founder of Christianity*. London: Collins, 1973.

"Donald Pleasence: Septimus Harding." IMDb. https://www.imdb.com/title/tt0086667/characters/nm0000587

Donne, John. *John Donne, A Selection of His Poems*. Edited by John Hayward. Harmondsworth: Penguin, 1950.

———. *The Complete English Poems*. London: Penguin, 1986.

———. *Complete Poetry and Selected Prose of John Donne*. New York: Random House, 2001.

Dorrien, Gary. "The Theological and the Political in Christianity, Socialism, and Modernity." Canopy Forum, June 15, 2021. https://canopyforum.org/2021/06/15/the-theological-and-the-political-in-christianity-socialism-and-modernity/.

Douglass, Frederick. *My Bondage and My Freedom*. New York: Miller, Orton & Mulligan, 1855.

Duffy, Eamon, ed. *The Heart in Pilgrimage: A Prayerbook for Catholic Christians*. London: Bloomsbury, 2013.

Dunn, James D. G. *Jesus' Call to Discipleship*. Cambridge: Cambridge University Press, 1992.

Durkheim, Emile. *The Elementary Forms of the Religious Life*. London: Allen and Unwin, 1915.

Edwards, George. *From Crow-Scaring to Westminster*. London: The Labour Party, 1922.

Eliot, George. *Adam Bede*. Harmondsworth: Penguin, 1985.

———. *Romola*. New York: Worthington, 1890.

———. *Middlemarch*. Harmondsworth: Penguin, 1965.

Eliot, T. S. *The Complete Poems and Plays*. London: Faber and Faber, 1969.

Emerson, Ralph Waldo. *Poems*. Boston: Houghton Mifflin, 1904.

Euronews. "Sins of the Fathers: Ireland's Sex Abuse Survivors." Nov 27, 2020. https://www.euronews.com/my-europe/2020/11/27/sins-of-the-fathers-ireland-s-sex-abuse-survivors.

Field, Clive. "Bible Literacy and Other News." British Religion in Numbers, Feb 7, 2014. http://www.brin.ac.uk/bible-literacy-and-other-news.

Fosdick, Harry Emerson. *On Being Fit to Live With*. London: SCM, 1947.

——— *What Is Vital in Religion*. London: SCM, 1956.

——— *The Living of These Days*. London: SCM, 1957.

Francis, Leslie, and Richter, Philip. *Gone for Good: Church-Leaving and Returning in the 21st Century*. Peterborough: Epworth, 2007.

Friedrich, Jim. "'The Terrible Work That Gives Life to the World'—A Good Friday Sermon." https://jimfriedrich.com/2021/04/02/the-terrible-work-that-gives-life-to-the-world-a-good-friday-sermon/.

Gardner, Helen, ed. *The New Oxford Book of English Verse, 1250–1950*. London: Oxford University Press, 1973.

Gibbon, Edward. *The History of the Decline and Fall of the Roman Empire, vol. 3*. New York: The Heritage Press, 1946.

Gifford, Paul. *The Plight of Western Religion: The Eclipse of the Other-Worldly*. London: C. Hurst, 2019.

# BIBLIOGRAPHY

Gladstone, W. E. *Church Principles Considered in Their Results*. London: John Murray, 1840.
Goodall, Jane, and Berman, Philip. *Reason to Hope*. New York: Warner, 2000.
Goulder, Michael. *A Tale of Two Missions*. London: SCM. 1994.
Green, S. J. D. *The Passing of Protestant England: Secularization and Social Change*. Cambridge: Cambridge University Press, 2012.
Greenlaw, Lavinia. *Minsk*. London: Faber and Faber, 2003.
Guite, Malcolm. "Daily Archives: December 14, 2016." https://malcolmguite.wordpress.com/2016/12/14/.
Hardy, Thomas. *Selected Poems*. London: Penguin, 1978.
———. *Tess of the D'Urbervilles*. Harmondsworth: Penguin, 1978.
Harries, Richard. *The Beauty and the Horror*. London: SPCK, 2016.
———. *Hearing God in Poetry*. London: SPCK, 2021.
Harrison, Michael, and Stuart-Clark, Christopher. *Oxford Book of Christmas Poems*. Oxford: Oxford University Press, 2005.
Hart, David Bentley. *The Experience of God*. New Haven: Yale University Press, 2013.
Hastings, Adrian. *Oliver Tomkins*. London: SPCK, 2001.
Hawking, Stephen, and Mlodinow, Leonard. *The Grand Design*. London: Bantam, 2010.
Hay, David. *Something There: The Biology of the Human Spirit*. London: Darton, Longman & Todd, 2006.
Healey, Denis. *The Time of My Life*. London: Penguin, 1990.
Hemingway, Ernest. *A Farewell to Arms*. New York: Simon and Schuster, 1997.
Herbert, George. *Herbert's Poems with his Country Parson*. London: Suttaby and Crosby, 1809.
———. *The English Poems of George Herbert*. London: Dent, 1974.
Hilton, Donald. *Table Talk*. London: United Reformed Church, 1998.
"History of Avebury Congregational Chapel, Avebury, Wiltshire." http://www.oodwooc.co.uk/ph_avebury_history2.htm.
Hobsbawm, Eric. *Age of Extremes: The Short Twentieth Century 1914–1991*. London: Abacus, 1995.
Hodgson, Ralph. *Poems*. London: MacMillan, 1917.
Holland, Tom. *Dominion: The Making of the Western Mind*. London: Little Brown, 2019.
Hoon, Paul. *The Integrity of Worship*. Nashville: Abingdon, 1971.
Houston, Brian. *You Need More Money*. N.p.: Trust Media Distribution, 2000.
Howard, Colin. *A History of Trinity Church Sutton, 1907–2007*. N.p.: Sutton, 2009.
Hughes, Langston. *Short Stories*. New York: Hill & Wang, 1996.
Huxley, Aldous. *The Devils of Loudun*. London: Chatto & Windus, 1922.
Ingalls, Monique M., and Amos Yong. *The Spirit of Praise, Music and Worship in Global Pentecostal-Charismatic Christianity*. University Park, PA: University of Pennsylvania Press, 2015.
James, Eric. *A Life of Bishop John A. T. Robinson*. London: Collins, 1987.
James, William. *Varieties of Religious Experience*. London: Longman, Green, 1917.
Jamieson, Christopher. *Finding the Language of Grace*. London: Bloomsbury, 2022.
Jenkins, David, and Rebecca Jenkins. *Free to Believe*. London: BBC Books, 1991.
Jenkins, Philip. *The New Faces of Christianity: Believing the Bible in the Global South*. New York: Oxford University Press, 2006.
Jenkins, Simon. *England's Thousand Best Churches*. London: Allen Lane, 1999.
———. *Europe's 100 Best Cathedrals*. London: Viking, 2021.

# BIBLIOGRAPHY

Jones, Arthur C. *Wade in the Water: The Wisdom of the Spirituals*. Maryknoll, NY: Orbis, 1993.
Kant, Immanuel. *Critique of Pure Reason*. Revised edition. Basingstoke: Palgrave, 2007.
Kavanagh, Patrick. *Collected Poems*. London: MacGibbon and Kee, 1964.
Kee, Alistair. *The Way of Transcendence: Christian Faith Without Belief in God*. Harmondsworth: Penguin, 1973.
Kennedy, John F. "Address before the 18th General Assembly of the United Nations." Sep 20, 1963. https://www.jfklibrary.org/archives/other-resources/john-f-kennedy-speeches/united-nations-19630920.
Kennedy, Roger. *American Churches*. New York: Stewart, Tabori & Chang, 1982.
Kenyon, Jane. *Collected Poems*. Saint Paul, MN: Graywolf Press, 2005.
*Songs of Fellowship*. Eastbourne: Kingsway Music, 1991.
Kipling, Rudyard. *Selected Poems*. Harmondsworth: Penguin, 1992.
Küng, Hans. *On Being a Christian*. Glasgow: Fount, 1978.
Lamott, Anne. *Plan B: Further Thoughts on Faith*. New York: Riverhead, 2005.
Larkin, Philip. *Collected Poems*. London: Marvell, 1988.
Lawrence, D. H. *The Rainbow*. Harmondsworth: Penguin, 1949.
Laqueur, Thomas Walter. *Religion and Respectability: Sunday Schools and Working Class Culture*. New Haven: Yale University Press, 1976.
L'Engle, Madeleine. *A Cry Like a Bell*. New York: Crown, 2000.
Loisy, Alfred. *L'Evangile et l'Eglise*. 5th French edition. Paris: hachette livre-bnf, 2018.
Long, Thomas G. *Beyond the Worship Wars*. Lanham, MD: Rowman & Littlefield, 2001.
Lloyd-Jones, Martyn. *Preaching and Preachers*. Grand Rapids: Zondervan, 2012.
Macarthur, Arthur. *Setting Up Signs*. London: United Reformed Church, 1997.
MacMullen, Ramsay. *Changes in the Roman Empire*. Princeton: N.p., 1990.
Mahler, Gustav. *Selected Letters of Gustav Mahler*. London: Faber, 1979.
Major, John. "John Major – Conference Speech Full Transcript." May 16, 2002. https://www.englishcathedrals.co.uk/latest-news/john-major-conference-speech-full-transcript.
Manning, Russell, ed. *The Cambridge Companion to Paul Tillich*. Cambridge: Cambridge University Press, 2009.
Marin, Andrew. "Communion Is about Equality." Apr 16, 2014. https://www.patheos.com/blogs/loveisanorientation/2014/04/communion-is-about-equality.
Martel, Frederic. *In the Closet of the Vatican*. London: Bloomsbury, 2019.
Meara, David. *A Passion for Places*. Stroud: Amberley, 2021.
Methodist Church. *Singing the Faith*. London: Hymns Ancient and Modern, 2011.
Miliband, Ralph. *Parliamentary Socialism*. London: Merlin Press, 1963.
Miller, Robert Moats. *Harry Emerson Fosdick: Preacher, Pastor, Prophet*. New York: Oxford University Press, 1985.
Milton, John. *Poetical Works*. Oxford: Oxford University Press, 1969.
Mladin Nathan. *The United Reformed Church: A Paradoxical Church at a Crossroads*. London: Theos, 2023.
Morris, Jeremy. *A People's Church*. London: Profile, 2022.
Muir, Edwin. *Selected Poems*. London: Faber and Faber, 1965.
Nicholson, Daniel & Lee, A. H. E., eds. *The Oxford Book of English Mystical Verse*. Oxford: Clarendon Press, 1917.

# BIBLIOGRAPHY

Niebuhr, Reinhold. *Man's Nature and His Communities: Essays on the Dynamics and Enigmas of Man's Personal and Social Existence.* New York: Charles Scribner's Sons, 1965.

Northwest Development Agency. *Faith in England's Northwest: The Contribution Made by Faith Communities to Civil Society in the Region.* Warrington: Northwest Development Agency, 2003.

Oates, Stephen. *Let the Trumpet Sound: The Life of Martin Luther King, Jr.* London: Search, 1982.

Oksenberg Rorty, Amelie, and James Schmidt. *Kant's Idea for a Universal History with a Cosmopolitan Aim.* Cambridge: Cambridge University Press, 2009.

Oldridge, D. *The Decline of the Supernatural in Tudor and Stuart England.* London: Routledge, 2016.

Otto, Rudolf. *The Idea of the Holy.* Harmondsworth: Penguin, 1959.

Paris, Peter, et al. *The History of the Riverside Church in the City of New York.* New York: New York University Press, 2004.

Parsons, Stephen. "When a Church Fails to Care. Facing Institutional Dishonesty." https://survivingchurch.org/2021/03/16/when-a-church-fails-to-care-facing-institutional-dishonesty/.

"'Pastoral Council' and the Collapse of the Catholic Faith in the Netherlands." National Catholic Register. https://www.ncregister.com/news/the-pastoral-council-and-the-collapse-of-the-catholic-faith-in-the-netherlands.

Percy, Martyn. *Clergy: The Origin of the Species.* London: Continuum, 2006.

———. *Power and the Church,* London, Cassell, 1998,

Pocock, W. F. *Designs for Churches & Chapels.* London: Spire, 2010.

Presbyterian Church in the USA. *Book of Common Worship.* Louisville: Westminster John Knox, 1994.

———. *Glory to God: The Presbyterian Hymnal.* Louisville: Westminster John Knox, 2013.

Rack, Henry. *Reasonable Enthusiast, John Wesley and the Rise of Methodism.* London: Epworth, 1989.

Rahner, Karl, et al., eds. *Karl Rahner in Dialogue: Conversations and Interviews, 1965–1982.* New York: Crossroad, 1986.

Rieder, Jonathan. "Songs of the Slaves: The Music of M.L.K.'s 'I Have a Dream.'" *New Yorker,* Aug 23, 2013.

Ritchie, Hannah, et al. "Hunger and Undernourishment." Our World in Data. https://ourworldindata.org/hunger-and-undernourishment.

Robinson, John A. T. *Honest to God.* London: SCM, 1963.

———. *The Difference in Being a Christian Today.* London: Fontana, 1972.

———. *The Human Face of God.* London. SCM, 1973.

———. *Can We Trust the New Testament?* Oxford: Mowbrays, 1977.

Rose, Michael. *Ugly as Sin: Why They Changed Our Churches from Sacred Spaces to Meeting Places.* Manchester, NH: Sophia Institute, 2002.

Rossetti, Christina. *The Complete Poems.* London: Penguin, 2001.

Rowntree, Seebohm, and Lavers, G. R. *English Life and Leisure.* London: Longmans and Green, 1951.

Searle, Joshua T. *Theology after Christendom: Forming Prophets for a Post-Christian World.* Eugene, OR: Cascade, 2018.

Shakespeare, William. *The Complete Works.* London: Murrays, 1977.

# BIBLIOGRAPHY

Sherry, Paul, ed. *The Riverside Preachers*. New York: Pilgrim, 1978.
Sittler, Joseph. *Grace Notes and Other Fragments*. Philadelphia: Fortress, 1981.
Smith, C. W. F. *The Jesus of the Parables*. Philadelphia: Westminster Press, 1948.
Solzhenitsyn, Aleksandr. *The Gulag Archipelago, 1918–1956*. London: Harvill, 2003.
Spitzer, Michael. *The Musical Human*. London: Bloomsbury, 2021.
Stallworthy, Jon. *The Penguin Book of Love Poetry*. London: Allen Lane, 1973.
Stopford, Philip W. J. *What Sweeter Music*. Oude Haske: De Haske, 2004.
"Superman As Jesus: Zack Snyder's Religious Imagery [The Director Project]." Mar 31, 2021. https://www.youtube.com/watch?v=U2BOXh7B4xc.
Tabor, J. A. *Nonconformist Protest against the Popery of Modern Dissent*. Colchester, 1863.
Taylor, Barbara Brown. *Leaving Church*. Norwich: Canterbury Press, 2011.
Taylor, Charles. *A Secular Age*. Cambridge, MA: The Belknap Press of Harvard University, 2007.
Temple, William. *Nature, Man and God*. London: Macmillan, 1940.
Tertullian, Quintus Septimius Florens. *The Apology*. Neuilly-sur-Seine: Ulan, 2012.
Thomas, R. S. *Collected Poems, 1945–1990*. London: Phoenix, 1995.
Thorne, Adriene. "To Be Continued by Rev. Adriene Thorne." Apr 9, 2023. https://www.youtube.com/watch?v=BzeQnM4vwpA.
Tickle, Phyllis. *The Great Emergence*. Grand Rapids: Baker, 2008.
Tillich, Paul. *The Shaking of the Foundations*. Harmondsworth: Pelican, 1962.
———. *The Boundaries of Our Being*. London: Fontana, 1973.
———. *Systematic Theology*, Vol. 1. London: SCM, 1978.
———. *Systematic Theology*, Vol. 2. Chicago: University of Chicago Press, 1957.
Traherne, Thomas. *Centuries of Meditations*. London: Christian Classics Ethereal Library, 1908.
Troeger, Thomas H. *Borrowed Light*. New York: Oxford University Press, 1994.
———. *Preaching While the Church is Under Reconstruction*. Nashville: Abingdon, 1999.
———. *Above the Moon Earth Rises*. Oxford: Oxford University Press, 2002.
———. *Wonder Reborn*. New York: Oxford University Press, 2010.
———. *The End of Preaching*. Nashville: Abingdon, 2018.
Trollope, Anthony. *Barchester Towers*. London: Dent, 1968.
Tyerman, Luke. *The Life and Times of the Rev. John Wesley*. Vol. 3. London: Hodder and Stoughton, 1871.
Trueheart, Charles. "Welcome to the Next Church." *The Atlantic*, Aug 1996.
Tutu, Desmond. *No Future Without Forgiveness*. London: Rider, 1999.
Vaughan, Henry. *Henry Vaughan: A Selection of His Poems*. Oxford: Oxford University Press, 1995.
United Methodist Church. *United Methodist Hymnal*. Nashville: United Methodist Publishing House, 1994.
United Reformed Church. *New Church Praise*. Edinburgh: Saint Andrews Press, 1979.
———. *Rejoice and Sing*. Oxford: Oxford University Press, 1991.
———. *Yearbook 2021*. London, 2021.
Vallely, Paul. *Philanthropy*. London: Bloomsbury, 2020.
Vance, J. D. *Hillbilly Elegy*. London: William Collins, 2016.
Vaughan, Henry. *The Complete Poems*. Edited by A. Rudrum. London: Penguin, 1995.
Vosper, Gretta. "Easter: Not Quite Yet." Apr 12, 2017. https://www.grettavosper.ca/easter-not-quite-yet/.
———. *With or Without God*. Toronto: HarperCollins, 2008.

# BIBLIOGRAPHY

Waddle, Ray. "Thomas H. Troeger: Between the Life of the Imagination and the Life of God." *Yale Divinity School News*, Mar 4, 2013.

Wagner, Tom. "Branding, Music, and Religion: Standardization and Adaptation in the Experience of the 'Hillsong Sound.'" In *Religions as Brands: New Perspectives on the Marketization of Religion and Spirituality*, edited by Jean-Claude Usunier and Jörg Stolz. Farnham: Ashgate, 2014.

Wakeling, Christopher. *Chapels of England: Buildings of Protestant Nonconformity*. Swindon: Historic England, 2017.

Wedderburn, A. J. M. *Beyond Resurrection*. London: SCM Press, 1999.

Wesley, John. "Letter to Dr. Rutherforth." *The Works of the Rev. John Wesley*, Vol. 8. New York: J. & J. Harper, 1827.

———. *The Works of the Reverend John Wesley, Vol. 7*. New York: Emory, 1831.

Wesley John, and Charles Wesley. *Hymns and Sacred Poems*. 1739.

Wheeler, Barbara. *Who Needs the Church*? Louisville: Geneva, 2004.

Whyte, William. *Unlocking the Church: The Lost Secrets of Victorian Sacred Space*. Oxford, Oxford University Press, 2017.

Williams, Rowan. *Lost Icons: Reflections on Cultural Bereavement*. London: T. & T. Clark, 2003.

Williams, Rowan. *Resurrection: Interpreting the Easter Gospel*. London: Darton, Longman & Todd, 2014

Wilson, A. N. *The Faber Book of Church and Clergy*. London, Faber and Faber, 1992.

Wind, James P., and James W. Lewis. *American Congregations, Volume Two: New Perspectives*. Chicago: University of Chicago Press, 1994.

Woodhead, Linda. "The Rise of No Religion in Britain." *Journal of the British Academy* 4 (2016) 245–61.

Wordsworth, William. *The Poetical Works of William Wordsworth*. London: Society for Promoting Christian Knowledge, 1900.

Wren, Brian. *Praying Twice: The Music and Words of Congregational Song*. Louisville: Westminster John Knox, 2000.

Yeats, W. B. *Selected Poetry*. London: Pan, 1974.

——— *The Collected Letters of W. B. Yeats, Vol. 1*. Edited by John Kelly. Oxford: Clarendon Press, 1986..

Yancey, Philip. "God's Funeral." *Christianity Today*, Sep 9, 2002. https://www.christianitytoday.com/ct/2002/september9/28.88.html.

# INDEX

Advent, 102
Albam, Tim, 95
Aldridge, Alan, 83
All Saints, 108
Aaronovitch, David, 97
Auden, W.H. 39–41, 103
Austen, Jane, 75–78, 165
   *Mansfield Park* 76–77, 165
Avebury United Reformed Church, 69–70, 80

Bach, Johann Sebastian, 55, 59, 105, 120, 136–37
   *Toccata and Fugue in D Minor* 136
Balls, Ed, 146–47
Baptism, Sacrament of, 119–11, 137–38
Barnes, Tony, xi
Barth, Karl, 19, 24–25, 162, 165
Bellah, Robert, 79, 165
Béres, Laura, 28, 165
Berger, Peter, 4, 143, 145–46, 165
Betjeman, John, 33–34, 41, 148, 151, 165
Bonhoeffer, Dietrich, 2, 10, 19, 54, 71, 159, 162–63, 165
Bradstreet, Anne, 111
Bruce, Steve, 11, 13, 95, 165
Bruckner, Anton, 98
Binfield, Clyde, xi, 43, 165
Blackmore, Suan, 143
Blake, William. 55, 138, 141
Borg, Marcus, 40
Botticelli, Sandro, 39, 146
Bradley, Ian, 118
Brightlingsea United Church, 80, 120

Brittain, Vera, 141
Brooks, David, 41
Browning, Elizabeth Barrett, 34
Browning, Robert, 137
Buchanan, John, 44, 53, 58, 110–11, 120, 130, 139, 159–61, 166
Bultmann, Rudolph, 48

Calvin, John, 1, 29, 53
Camroux, Eleanor, xi
Camroux, Margaret, xi, 158
Camroux, Mark, 125, 138, 142
Camroux, Martin, vii–ix, 39, 166
Camroux, Michael, xi, 12
Camroux, Olwen, 160
Carroll, James, 136
Carter, Sydney, 46, 49, 52
Castle Hill, United Reformed Church, Ipswich, 36–37
Chagall. Marc, 37
Chappel United Reformed Church, 152
Chaucer, Geoffrey, 23, 27–28, 52, 166
Chesterton, G.K. 26, 166
Christ Church URC Port Sunlight, 26
Christmas, 42, 90, 102–3
Church in Wales, 8
Church of England, 6, 8–9, 21. 75, 96, 166
Coffin, William Sloane, xi, 60, 125, 136, 141, 161
Conalty, Julie, 22
Congregational Union in England and Wales, 6, 166
Constable, John, 106
Cooke, Roger, xi

# INDEX

Copeland, Keneth, 116–17
Corbett, Elsa, 80–81
Cornick, David, xi, 30, 166
Covid, 10, 13, 96, 131, 140, 146, 154
Cox, Brian, 143
Cox, Harvey, 51, 54, 166
Crashaw, Richard, 57
Crossman, Richard, 90
Crossman, Samuel, 49
Cubitt, James, 33, 166

Dalí, Salvador, 58, 166
Davis, Ellen, 29
Dawkins, Richard, 47, 144–45, 166
Dickens, Charles, 29
Dickinson, Emily, 15, 87–88, 120, 125–26, 128, 167
  *Hope is the thing with feathers*, 120
Didion, Joan, 56
Donne, John, 124–26, 167
Dorrien, Gary, 19, 167
Douglass, Frederick, 85
Dunn, James, 73, 167
Durkheim, Emile, 83–84, 91, 94, 97, 153, 167

Eagleton, Terry, 144
Easter, 63–567, 106–7, 120, 128–29, 155–56
Edwards, George, 153
Elgar, Edward, 112, 146
  *Dream of Gerontius*, 146
Eliot, George, 75–77, 158–59
  *Adam Bede*, 77–167
  *Middlemarch*, 75–76, 159
Eliot, T.S. 72, 102
Emerson, Ralph Waldo, 146
Eucharist, 109

Fairland United Reformed Church, Wymondham, 153
Fosdick, Harry Emerson, 30, 33, 48, 100–101, 122–25, 128, 134, 162, 167
Fourth Presbyterian Church, Chicago, 44, 120, 139

Freemantle United Reformed Church, Southampton, xi, 1, 3, 8, 78, 87, 90, 93–94, 157–58
Freud, Sigmund, 137
Friedrich, Jim, 67, 167
Funerals, 70, 87–88, 90, 93, 109, 112, 138

Gaskell, Elizabeth, 75, 77
Gates, Bill, 101
Gifford, Paul, 10, 116–17, 167
Gladstone, William, 38
Gleed, Geoffrey, xi, 120
Gomes, Peter, 63
Goodall, Jane, 136–37
Goodwin, Gail, 130
Graham, Billy, 93
Gray, John, 145
Green, Fred Pratt, 42, 98, 133
Green, S.J.D. 7–8, 168
Grünewald, Mathias, 58, 105

Hall, Douglas John, 157
Hamilton, Jo, 95
Handel, George Frideric, 55, 59, 106, 120, 136
  *Messiah*, 59, 120, 128, 136
Harleston Congregational Church, 29, 31
Harvest Festivals, 102, 107
Hawking, Stephen, 144, 146
Healey, Denis, 76, 168
Houston, Brian, 117, 127
Huxley, Aldous, 124
Bentley Hart, David, 65–66, 168
Harris, Dan, 115
Haugen, Marty, 59, 62, 120
Hay, David, 40, 168
Hayward, John, 8, 167
Heaney, Seamus, 9
Hemingway, Ernest, 140–41
Herbert, George, 44–45, 86–87, 122, 132, 168
Hillsong Church, 113–15, 118, 127
Hilton, Donald, 110, 123, 168
Holland, Tom, 54, 59, 93–94, 144–45, 168
Hughes, Langston, 105

# INDEX

Hull University Christian Association, 68, 71–72

Immanuel United Reformed Church, Swindon, xi, 96, 104–5, 125
Ingallsis, Monique, 113

James, William, 38, 168
Jenkins, David, 65, 160, 168
Jenkins, Simon, 32, 35–36, 41, 137, 168
Jesus Passim
   And the Church, 17, 46–47, 67–68, 73–74
   Birth Stories, 56–57
   Crucified God. 57–62
   Ethics, 51–55
   Human Face of God, 55–56, 62
   Parables, 49, 51–53
   Place in my Life, 48–51
   Resurrection, 63–67, 127–8
Jones, Arthur C. 85
Jones, Bert, 70, 80
Jones, Martyn Lloyd, 130
Jonson, Ben, 88
Julian of Norwich, 62

Kant, Immanuel, 56, 145, 150
Kavanagh, Patrick, 9, 169
Kee, Alistair, 2
Kennedy, President John F. 71
Kennedy, Roger, 44, 169
King, Martin Luther, 3, 71, 85, 93, 123, 162
Kipling, Rudyard, 105, 107, 169

Lamott, Anne, 82
Larkin, Philip. 2, 5–6, 8, 13, 25–26, 34, 41, 108, 149–51, 154, 157, 163, 169
Lawrence, David xi
Lawrence, D.H. 28
Lent, 103–4
Lewitt, Anne, xi
Lincoln Cathedral, 28, 143
Lion Walk Church, Colchester, 33–34, 36, 80
Long, Thomas, 118
Luther, Martin, 10, 19, 156

Macarthur, Arthur, 4–5, 169
MacPherson, Ian xi
McCowen, Alec, 47–48
McDonald, Iain, 75
McGregor, Neil, 78
MacNeice, Louis, 111
Mahler, Gustav, 66–67, 169
Major, John, 151–52
Mamet, David, 124
Mansfield College, Oxford, 1, 30, 34–35, 48
Marx, Karl, 24, 56
Mary, mother of Jesus, 17, 57, 64
Mead, Frank, 48, 100–1
Methodist Church, xii, 8, 14, 21–22, 34, 61, 72, 76–77
Michelangelo, 137
Miliband, Ralph, 153–54
Milton, John, 23, 55, 92, 104, 147, 153, 169
Mount Bures, 151–52
Muir, Edwin, 31, 169
Myers, Sydney, 156

Newman, John Henry, 112
Nietzsche, Friedrich, 53–54
Niebuhr, Reinhold, 24, 54, 170
Notre Dame Cathedral, Paris, 136–37
Nouwen, Henri, 7

Otto, Rudolph, 26, 170
Owen, Wilfred, 107
Oxford, beauty of, 29–30

Parris, Matthew, 144
Peabody, George, 89
Peel, David, vii– xi
Percy, Martyn, 115
Peterson, Eugene, 75
Pocock, W.F. 31, 170
Powell, Enoch, 67
Presbyterian Church in the USA, 100
Presbyterian Church of England, 4, 140
Price, George, 54
Prosperity Theology, 116–17, 127
Pugin, Augustus, 32, 137

Reformed Theology, 120–21, 161–2
Remembrance Sunday, 107

# INDEX

Reeves, Rachel, 80
Riverside Church, New York, xi, 3–31, 34, 120, 122–23, 125, 128–29
Roberts, Oral, 116
Robinson, Gene, 74
Robinson, John, 2–3, 39–40, 49, 55, 71, 162, 170
Roman Catholic Church, 2–3, 5, 7–8, 15, 18, 20, 71, 111, 122, 161
Roosevelt, Theodore, 101
Rossetti, Christina, 155–56
Rowntree, Joseph, 89
Rowntree, Seebohm, 7–8, 93, 170
Rutter, John, 120

St. Denys, Paris, 28
St. John the Baptist, Mount Bures, 151
Sy. Mary the Virgin, Dedham, 106
St. Stephen Bures, 32
Searl, Joshua T. 150
Secularization, vii, 8–13, 34, 20, 95, 160
Sewell, Bill, 80
Sex Abuse in Churches, 19–22
Shakespeare. William, 22, 141, 153, 170
Sheppard, David, 96
Sheppard, Dick, 125
Sherry, Paul, H. 93, 122, 125, 171
Shrub End Congregational Church, 48, 68, 100–1
Simon and Garfunkel, 71
Sledge, Sharlande, 27
Solzhenitsyn, Alexander, 24, 171
Spitzer, Michael, 88–89

Tabor, J.A. 33, 36, 171
Taylor, Barbara Brown, 74–75
Taylor, Charles, 126
Theresa, Mother, 19, 59, 62
Thomas, Dylan, 119
Thomas, R.S. 25, 99
Thompson, Emma, 138–39
Thorne, Adriene, l28–9
Tickle, Phyliss, 161
Tilby, Angela, 43–44
Tillich, Paul, 10, 19, 38–39, 66, 162, 171
Traherne, Thomas, 60, 171

Trinity United Reformed and Methodist Church, Sutton, xi, 37, 42–43, 80–81, 90, 106, 110, 120, 132–33
Trinity With Palm Grove United Reformed and Methodist Church, Birkenhead, xi, 142
Troeger, Thomas H, 55–56, 98, 120–21, 126, 133, 171
Trollope, Anthony, 75–76, 119, 124, 171
   *Barchester Towers* 76, 119, 124
Trueheart, Charles, 37, 171
Trump, Donald, 18, 93, 117, 127
Turner, Victoria, 162
Tutu, Desmond, 54, 72, 93, 162, 171

Uffington, 26
United Reformed Church (URC), vii, 3, 6, 8, 14–15, 17, 20–22, 35, 38, 79, 96, 104–5, 152, 158, 160
Updike, John, 63–64

Vance, J.D. 88- 89
Vaughan, Henry, 106
Villarreal, Sandi, 37–38
Vosper, Gretta, 129

Wagner, Tom, 114
Wallis, Jim, 52, 60
Watts, Isaac, 49, 85–86, 120
Weatherhead, Leslie, 48, 123, 126–27, 129
Weil, Simone, 143
Welby, Justin, 9–12, 75, 155
Wesley, John, 31, 73–74, 127, 162, 172
Wheeler, Barbara, 16, 172
Whyte, William, 32–33, 172
Williams, Rowan, 66, 119
Williams, Vaughan, 108
Wilson, A.N., 13, 172
Winchester Cathedral, 144, 146
Woodhead, Linda, 11, 74, 165, 172
Wordsworth, William, 10, 138, 172
Wren, Brian, 115, 117, 120, 172
Wymondham College, 1, 15, 123, 153, 156

Yeats, W.B. 29–30, 123, 172,

Zwingli, Huldrych, 103

www.ingramcontent.com/pod-product-compliance
Lightning Source LLC
Chambersburg PA
CBHW072132160426
43197CB00012B/2081